MISTER

MISTER
Answers to the questions you're afraid to ask

Dr. Michael Stokes, LPC

Copyright © 2026 Dr. Michael Stokes. All rights reserved.

No part of this publication shall be reproduced, transmitted, or sold in whole or in part in any form without prior written consent of the author, except as provided by the United States of America copyright law. Any unauthorized usage of the text without express written permission of the publisher is a violation of the author's copyright and is illegal and punishable by law. All trademarks and registered trademarks appearing in this guide are the property of their respective owners.

For permission requests, write to the publisher, addressed "Attention: Permissions Coordinator," at the address below.

Publish Your Purpose
141 Weston Street, #155
Hartford, CT, 06141

The opinions expressed by the Author are not necessarily those held by Publish Your Purpose.

Ordering Information: Quantity sales and special discounts are available on quantity purchases by corporations, associations, and others. For details, contact the author at DrMike@MisterHealth.com.

Edited by: Maria Chapman
Cover design by: Barb Pritchard
Typeset by: Medlar Publishing Solutions Pvt Ltd., India

ISBN: 979-8-88797-208-4 (hardcover)
ISBN: 979-8-88797-209-1 (paperback)
ISBN: 979-8-88797-210-7 (ebook)

Library of Congress Control Number: 2025915822

First edition, January 2026.

The information contained within this book is strictly for informational purposes. The material may include information, products, or services by third parties. As such, the Author and Publisher do not assume responsibility or liability for any third-party material or opinions. The publisher is not responsible for websites (or their content) that are not owned by the publisher. Readers are advised to do their own due diligence when it comes to making decisions.

Publish Your Purpose is a hybrid publisher of non-fiction books. Our mission is to elevate the voices often excluded from traditional publishing. We intentionally seek out authors and storytellers with diverse backgrounds, life experiences, and unique perspectives to publish books that will make an impact in the world. Do you have a book idea you would like us to consider publishing? Please visit PublishYourPurpose.com for more information.

To
all of my brave clients
who showed up in my office and were vulnerable
and allowed me to watch their growth over the years.

CONTENTS

ACKNOWLEDGMENTS … xiii

INTRODUCTION … xv

Part I
You Deserve Better Sex

CHAPTER 1
Why Do I Struggle with Sex So Much? … 3

CHAPTER 2
Are My Sexual Fantasies Normal? … 21

CHAPTER 3
Is It Okay to Like This? Understanding Kinks and BDSM … 35

CHAPTER 4
What's the Deal with Porn? … 45

CHAPTER 5
How Much Masturbation Is Too Much? — 61

CHAPTER 6
Am I Gay? Straight? Bi? Does It Matter? — 81

CHAPTER 7
How Do I Figure Out What I Really Want in My Sex Life? — 95

CHAPTER 8
Why Do I Sometimes Want Sex and Other Times I Don't? — 101

CHAPTER 9
Are There Other Places I Can Experience Pleasure Other Than My Penis? — 113

Part 2
Demystifying Partnered Sex

CHAPTER 10
What Makes a Sexual Relationship Healthy? — 127

CHAPTER 11
How Do I Talk to My Partner About Sex Without It Being Awkward? — 143

CHAPTER 12
What's the Point of Partnered Sex? — 157

CHAPTER 13
How Can I Deal with Being Rejected? — 167

Part 3
Sex Challenges

CHAPTER 14
Should I Be Using Sex Toys and Other Enhancers? — 179

CHAPTER 15
How Can I Fix Erectile Problems? 191

CHAPTER 16
Why Do I Get So Nervous About Sex and How Can I Stop? 211

CHAPTER 17
What Can I Do About Performance Anxiety? 231

PART 4

MINDFUL SEX FOR LIFE

CHAPTER 18
What Is Sensate Focus? 249

CHAPTER 19
What Do I Really Care About When It Comes to Sex? 265

CONCLUSION 281

AUTHOR'S NOTE 287

ABOUT THE AUTHOR 289

ACKNOWLEDGMENTS

Writing *Mister* has been one of the most meaningful projects of my career and my life. This book stands on the shoulders of many.

To my mentors, teachers, and colleagues in the field of sex therapy: thank you for your courage, your vision, and your willingness to challenge cultural taboos in pursuit of truth, healing, and sexual wellness. You laid the foundation that made this work possible. I am grateful for the generations of sex therapists before me who did the brave, often thankless work that now allows others, myself included, to carry the torch forward with clarity and compassion.

To those who contributed directly to the publication of this book—editors, designers, proofreaders, and publishing partners—thank you for your creativity, insight, and tireless commitment to producing a book that reflects the depth and nuance of these conversations.

To my clients and readers: thank you for your vulnerability, honesty, and trust. You taught me as much as I hope this book teaches you.

To my family—Chris Ritton-Stokes, Charlotte Ritton-Stokes, and Hudson Ritton-Stokes—you are my heart. Chris, your unwavering belief in me and this work gave me the courage to say what needed to be said. Charlotte and Hudson, your curiosity, laughter, and love remind me why authenticity and empathy matter. Thank you for giving me the space to be both Dad and Dr. Stokes.

This book is for every man who's ever wondered if he's the only one asking these questions—you're not. And now, you have a place to start.

With deepest gratitude,

Dr. Michael Stokes

INTRODUCTION

I never set out to become a sex therapist.

When I first started my career in therapy, I noticed something strange: clients wanted to talk about sex, but their previous therapists had either changed the topic or referred them out because it wasn't their area of expertise. The message was clear—sex was not an appropriate conversation for the therapy room.

Except, sex is a huge part of what makes us human. It is part of how we identify ourselves, straight, gay, bisexual, etc. Sex affects our mental health and our physical health. Sex is an integral part of our most personal relationships (which are often the ones we want to discuss in therapy).

I didn't want to be another therapist who shied away from these discussions. If my clients needed a safe, nonjudgmental space to talk about sex, I wanted to be that space. The more I talked about it, the more I realized just how much men struggled with sex—not just the physical aspects but also the emotional, psychological, and relational complexities that come with it.

That realization forced me to confront my own knowledge gaps. I had spent nine years in school to become a therapist—earning the highest level of education I could get—and yet, not a single course had covered sex. How could I help clients navigate their sexual concerns when our entire field had largely ignored this critical aspect of human well-being? How could I expect other therapists to navigate sexual health conversations if sex was never on the agenda?

So, I went back to school—this time in a different way. I pursued professional development in sex therapy, obtained certification, and immersed myself in research and clinical training. I thought I already had a good grasp of what it meant to be sex-positive, open, and nonjudgmental. But I was in for a wake-up call.

As I examined my own beliefs about sex, I realized how much guilt and shame had shaped my views. I had internalized messages from my family, religion, colleagues, and society without ever questioning them. I believed body image concerns were exclusive to women and gay men—I didn't realize straight men struggled with them too. I thought erectile dysfunction was a problem for men over 60—I had no idea how many young, healthy men dealt with it. I assumed monogamous, heterosexual relationships were the default standard—I had never explored the vast spectrum of relationship structures that exist.

These beliefs didn't align with my core values of being inclusive and open and not being judgmental. I had to challenge and rewrite them. If I wanted to help men navigate their sexuality in a way that was free of shame, I first had to do the work myself.

This book is the result of that journey. It reflects the questions I had to answer for myself and the ones I hear from clients every day. Some of the questions are from the guy I met at the gym. When I told him I was a sex therapist he said, "Can I ask you some questions?" It's the book I wish existed when I first started this work—and the one I hope will provide men with the answers they've been searching for.

I wrote *Mister* to be an informative, practical guide for men who want more—more confidence, more fulfillment, more connection in their sex lives. Whether you're struggling with performance anxiety, questioning your fantasies, rethinking your porn use, or just looking for a fresh perspective on sex, this book is for you.

There's so much misinformation about sex floating around—whether in locker rooms, outdated sex ed classes, or the cesspool of advice on the internet. A brief internet search for "porn use," for example, returns everything from "Porn is not a problem" to "If you watch porn your penis is going to fall off." How are men who want answers supposed to find them? My goal is to cut through the noise and offer research-backed, judgment-free, sex-positive guidance.

Before you read on, I want to define the term *sex-positive* for you. You'll encounter people who claim to be sex-positive, especially if you're seeking help from clinicians and therapists. I want you to know how I define it so you can evaluate for yourself if it's a view that works for you. Sex-positive means believing that sex is a normal, healthy part of life and that people should feel free to talk about it, explore it, and enjoy it—without shame or judgment. It means respecting everyone's choices, as long as they are safe, consensual, and respectful.

In simple terms, it's about:

- No shame: Sex isn't dirty or bad, and no one should feel guilty about their desires.
- Consent first: Everyone involved should fully agree to what's happening.
- All choices are valid: Whether someone wants lots of sex, no sex, or anything in between, it's okay.
- Sex education matters: Knowing about safety, pleasure, and health makes sex better.
- Respecting diversity: Different relationships, identities, and preferences are all valid.

Basically, being sex-positive means embracing an open, respectful, and informed attitude toward sex and relationships. I've included a guide for finding an AASECT-certified sex therapist at the end of this book. If, at any point while you're reading, you think finding a therapist to help you navigate your concerns is the right move for you, I encourage you to use the guide to help you search for the right fit.

If there's one thing I want you to take away from this book, it's this: You are not broken. Your concerns, your struggles, your questions—they are valid, and they have answers. Let's explore them together.

DR. MIKE'S AUTONOMOUS SEXUALITY MODEL

When I started working with men in a sex therapy capacity, I saw certain themes emerge with the questions they asked. That's what most of this book is. But I also saw themes emerge in how I responded, and how those responses helped my clients.

After more than a decade, I formulated this learning into the Autonomous Sexuality Model. This model consists of four principles that guide conversations about and decisions related to your sexual health.

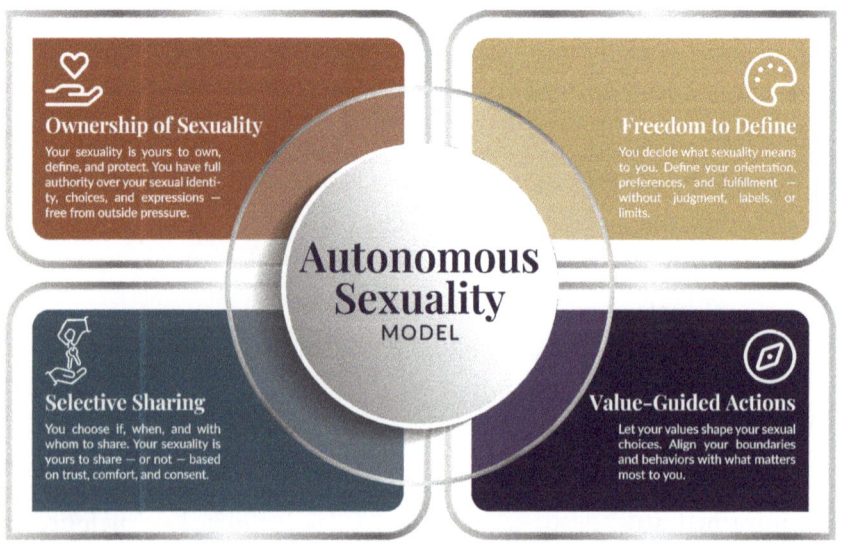

1. **Ownership of Sexuality**
   - Your sexuality belongs to you.
   - This principle asserts that you are the sole proprietor of your sexuality. It emphasizes that your sexual identity, preferences, and expressions are inherently yours and should not be influenced or dictated by external pressures. It encourages an understanding that you have the ultimate authority over your sexual choices.
2. **Freedom to Define**
   - You get to define ALL aspects of your sexuality.
   - Every individual has the right to explore and define what sexuality means to them without judgment or coercion. This includes determining one's sexual orientation, preferences, and what sexual fulfillment looks like. This component promotes the idea that defining one's sexuality is a personal journey that should be guided by self-reflection and personal understanding.
3. **Selective Sharing**
   - You can share your sexuality as you wish and with whom you wish.
   - This aspect of the model supports the idea that sharing your sexuality is a choice that should be respected by others. It highlights the importance of consent and mutual respect in all sexual interactions. You have the autonomy to decide if, when, and with whom to share your sexual self, based on your comfort and trust levels.
4. **Value-Guided Actions**
   - Your values guide your sexual decisions and boundaries.
   - Your personal values and ethics play a crucial role in shaping your sexual decisions and setting boundaries. This component stresses the importance of aligning your sexual behaviors with your values, which helps foster a sense of integrity and satisfaction in your sexual relationships. It also supports

the development of healthy boundaries that protect and respect your well-being and that of others.

As you read the following chapters, I urge you to consider each of these four principles in relation to what I share with you. How can you make decisions that center your values, your autonomy, and your desires, and how can you share those with other people who have a stake in your sex life?

**All client names and personal details have been altered to protect their identity, but the stories and struggles I share are very real.

PART 1

You Deserve Better Sex

CHAPTER 1

WHY DO I STRUGGLE WITH SEX SO MUCH?

The most common problem men have with partnered or solo sex is getting out of their head, into their body, and enjoying the experience without worry, anxiety, or stress.

Steve walked into my office for his first appointment frustrated about having sex with his partner. Like most guys in today's fast-paced world, he struggles with being in the moment. This impacts both his work and personal lives, making it challenging to find any escape from the madness inside his head. After a lot of deliberation, Steve decided to consult a sex therapist—and reached out to me directly.

After some prompting, he went into detail about one of their most recent sexual encounters. It started off seemingly harmless—the couple was going out to dinner one summer evening, the type that feels romantic for no particular reason. Steve was worried about how he'd initiate sex later on and kept looking for signs his partner was interested.

"What are all the ways I could go about initiating sex?" he thought as they headed to the restaurant. "Do I need to do anything to set the mood?" "Should we cuddle, shower, or dance in the living room?" "Once we get past that, how are we going to start having sex?" "How long is foreplay going to be?" "Will she want me to go down on her?"

Dinner provides a welcome distraction from life's daily stressors and allows Steve and his partner the opportunity to enjoy each other's company. Over a multi-course meal, a few glasses of wine, and an ambience equivalent to the strongest aphrodisiacs, the pair head home in lively spirits.

They head upstairs to get ready for bed. While undressing, it dawns upon Steve—this is the moment to go for it!

Not one to waste time, he quickly initiates with a soft kiss, getting a green light from his partner. The couple continues kissing, growing more passionate with each moment. Steve, though, can't seem to stay in the moment and starts planning his next moves step-by-step like a flow chart.

"Ok, we've been kissing for one minute 45 seconds, then oral, maybe some light foreplay, then onto penetration . . ." His brain spins.

(If you're laughing at Steve's watching the clock, know he isn't the only one who sits in my office and says something similar.)

Suddenly, in the middle of performing oral sex, his thoughts take a turn for the worse. "Is my partner enjoying this? I'm not hearing anything. Is this taking too long? Is my partner bored?"

Attempting to get past those intrusive thoughts, Steve decides to move on to intercourse, trying to talk himself through it, telling himself things like don't come too fast, don't mess up the rhythm, don't be too aggressive.

He orgasms, or they both do, and then it's over.

To Steve, it feels like it was a win, kind of. But deep down inside, he can't help thinking something is missing. He doesn't have a sense of fulfillment.

After Steve describes this evening in my office, I pause for a moment.

"Did you enjoy it?" I ask him.

He hesitates, then says, "I think so. I mean, I did come."

When I try to get him to call out specific things that felt good, he mentions his partner's pleasure or focuses on logistics. "It lasted twenty minutes, and I went down on her first."

"I want to follow that thought," I prompt, hoping to get more out of him.

"What do you mean?"

"Can you elaborate a little bit more?"

"My partner seemed to like it," he responds.

"Anything else?"

"I was able to stay hard the whole time."

None of his responses focused on *his* pleasure or what he enjoyed about the experience. Why?

He couldn't stay present at the moment. He was overly focused on . . .

Logistics.

Timing.

Function.

I let Steve know what I noticed about his focus on the how-to's of sex. "What happens if you don't know what's going to happen next? What if you just show up? What if there is no flowchart and it's messy, clunky, clumsy, and you don't get it right?"

"I don't know what to expect, too much could go wrong. She might decide she wants to stop if I don't do a good job, or she might say no altogether."

So many men who come into my office describe partnered sex and solo sex in terms of logistics and function. Their penis works or it doesn't, they fool around before "the real thing" or they just "get right to it" (the real thing, and "it" referring to the penis-in-vagina sex we learn about in sex education classes).

They worry that if they don't do things perfectly their partner will reject them. They worry they may not recover from that rejection. They worry that their penis won't get erect, or stay erect, or be erect enough. All this worry and anxiety not only hampers their enjoyment of the experience, but their partners notice too.

Has your partner ever said they feel like you're somewhere else during sex? What about asking you for more connection? If so, it's likely because they can tell you're in your head instead of in the moment with them.

BEING IN YOUR HEAD AFFECTS SOLO SEX TOO

Another client, Matt, expressed concerns about masturbating during our consultation call.

"I feel like I'm masturbating too much. But I'm not even enjoying it. I just do it quickly to get to the end, so I can come. Sometimes It's hard to get hard, sometimes it's hard for me to come, and sometimes I come really fast. I can only masturbate while watching porn."

Right away, I knew we had an "in his head, not in his body" problem.

Being too in your head during solo sex leads to mindless masturbation: just masturbating to masturbate.

STRESSED AT WORK? MASTURBATE TO RELIEVE STRESS

Worried about money? Masturbate to alleviate the worry for a moment.

Trouble sleeping? Masturbate so you can get to sleep.

Of course, orgasm produces chemicals in your brain that help you feel more relaxed, a bit sleepy, and able to chill out—but if you're using orgasm as your sole means of relaxing, we've got a problem.

If you're like Matt, the goal of masturbating is to disconnect from your body, but that's the opposite of what your sexuality should be for you. Your sexuality should help you connect to your body.

In our conversations I learned that Matt had a previous partner who shamed him for masturbating and felt he should only be having sex with them. He also grew up hearing religious messaging that masturbation is wrong or bad. Add in societal messaging such as the #NoFap movement, an internet movement that originated in a Reddit thread[1] and touted abstinence from masturbation, orgasms, and pornography as a

---

[1] Reddit. (2019). *R/NoFap*. https://www.reddit.com/r/NoFap/.

solution to sexual health issues,[2] and Matt needed some masturbation intervention.

I get more in depth into a discussion of masturbation in later chapters, but here, let's just discuss how mindfulness can impact your partnered and solo sex.

WHERE DOES THIS DISCONNECTION AND WORRY COME FROM?

Steve reported learning about sex mostly from watching porn. Sure, his sex education classes in high school went over the mechanics, but technique mattered, and he used porn to try to figure out what women want in bed.

Matt experienced intense shaming from previous relationships when it came to his masturbation habit, and he remembers learning in church that masturbation was evil and would send him to hell.

These men, like so many others who sit in my office, learned about sex in all the wrong places and never learned that they need to talk to their partners about sex (in detail) or that it was okay to explore. Men are taught that they need to perform well in bed (and elsewhere). They hear that an enduring, rock-hard erection is the measure of their manhood, and that they should be "ready to go" at any moment.

None of this is true.

Sex is more than logistics, function, and orgasms. Men have been missing out on the good stuff. It's time to dial back the anxiety, peel back the curtain, and figure out what sex is really all about.

---

[2] Zimmer, F., & Imhoff, R. (2020). Abstinence from masturbation and hypersexuality. *Archives of Sexual Behavior, 49*(4), 1333–1343. https://doi.org/10.1007/s10508-019-01623-8.

WHAT DO WE *DO* ABOUT IT?

Whether you're working on getting out of your head and into your body during solo or partnered sex, the process is the same. I've developed The Mister Method after working with men over several years as a certified therapist, and then as a certified *sex* therapist. Mindfulness reduces sexual anxiety and performance anxiety.[3,4] We explore many pieces of this framework in greater detail in coming chapters, but this overview should serve as a starting point for your self-discovery and your new sex education.

THE MISTER METHOD FOR MINDFUL SEX

Mindfulness	Intimacy	Somatic Awareness	Trust	Embodiment	Reconnection
Sex starts in the mind. Mindfulness helps men move from performance to presence.	Real intimacy requires vulnerability — emotional, not just physical.	Your body holds the answers.	Trust in yourself, your partner, and the process.	To be embodied is to be fully in your body — not stuck in your head.	This journey is about returning to yourself.
• Learn to notice your thoughts without judgment	• Share a fear with your partner	• Notice where you tense up during arousal or stress	• Trust that you're enough — even if you struggle with ED or desire issues	• Move your body (yoga, dance, walking)	• Reconnect with your purpose
• Ground your body before intimacy	• Talk about a past experience that shaped your view of sex	• Learn to relax your pelvic floor and engage your senses	• Trust that your body will respond in time	• Develop a daily connection to pleasure that isn't just sexual	• Reconnect with your sexuality
• Use breathwork to stay present in the moment	• Touch without the goal of penetration	• Practice non-goal-based touch (i.e., massage, sensual exploration)	• Trust that it's okay to slow down	• Reclaim self-pleasure as a way to explore, not just release	• Reconnect with your inner voice, not society's noise

---

[3] Jaderek, I., & Lew-Starowicz, M. (2019). A systematic review on mindfulness meditation-based interventions for sexual dysfunctions. *The Journal of Sexual Medicine*, *16*(10), 1581–1596. https://doi.org/10.1016/j.jsxm.2019.07.019.

[4] Krieger, J. F., Kristensen, E., Marquardsen, M., Ofer, S., Mortensen, E. L., & Giraldi, A. (2023). Mindfulness in sex therapy and intimate relationships: A feasibility and randomized controlled pilot study in a cross-diagnostic group. *Sexual Medicine*, *11*(3), qfad033. https://doi.org/10.1093/sexmed/qfad033.

Mindfulness

Sex starts in the mind. Mindfulness helps men move from performance to presence.

- Learn to notice your thoughts without judgment
- Ground your body before intimacy
- Use breathwork to stay present in the moment

Try this: Before sex or masturbation, pause for three slow, deep breaths. Say to yourself, "I am here now."

How you feel will show up during sex. If you've had an unresolved argument from the night before, are stressed at work, or haven't had enough sleep, these emotional states will affect your sexual experience. Before you engage in sex, take a moment to check in with your emotions. Acknowledge how you're feeling and ensure you can be present for your partner. This step is crucial for creating a connected and fulfilling sexual experience.

When I'm working with men, we often spend a significant amount of time here. Mindfulness improves your entire life, not just your sex life, especially if you practice it in other areas. This could mean reducing the amount of time you spend multi-tasking, paying more attention to your food when you eat, focus on your partner when they talk to you, and really feel how your body moves when you exercise.

Intimacy

Real intimacy requires vulnerability—emotional, not just physical.

- Share a fear with your partner
- Talk about a past experience that shaped your view of sex
- Touch without the goal of penetration

Intimacy is connection, not performance.

When you practice intimacy in other areas of your life, you have better sex. Your partner wants to have sex with you. They want to be with you. Focus on all the reasons it can go right. Think about why they are in front of you, why they want to be vulnerable with you, and why they want to experience pleasure together.

Somatic Awareness

Your body holds the answers.

- Notice where you tense up during arousal or stress
- Learn to relax your pelvic floor and engage your senses
- Practice non-goal-based touch (i.e., massage, sensual exploration)

Slowing down is vital for fulfilling sex. That's not to say a quickie in the guest room during a party isn't fun, but if quickies are the only sex you're having, you're missing out on the intensity of true connection. If you want better sex, with yourself or your partner, intimacy is the place to start.

Trust

Trust in yourself, your partner, and the process.

- Trust that you're enough—even if you struggle with ED or desire issues
- Trust that your body will respond in time
- Trust that it's okay to slow down

Intrusive thoughts will come into your head, and that's okay. Shake them off and focus on positive affirmations. Remember, your partner wants you to be present. They want you—all of you. They are choosing to have sex with you intentionally. Remind yourself that you are a good partner, a good lover, and a good sex partner.

Embodiment

To be embodied is to be fully in your body—not stuck in your head.

- Move your body regularly (yoga, dance, walking—anything that gets you in your skin)
- Develop a daily connection to pleasure that isn't just sexual
- Reclaim self-pleasure as a way to explore, not just release

Bring yourself back to the present moment by focusing on your senses.[5] What can you see, hear, touch, taste, and smell? Engage with these sensations to deepen your connection and enjoyment.

- **Focus on What You Can Touch:** What does it feel like? What part of your partner's body do you enjoy touching the most? Pay attention to these sensations.
- **Focus on What You Hear:** What do you hear? Can you hear your partner moan? Can you hear what they are saying? Focus on these sounds to affirm you are in the moment.
- **Focus on What You See:** Scan your partner's body. Take a look into their eyes. Focus your sight on the parts of their body that heighten your arousal.
- **Focus on What You Can Taste:** Concentrate on kissing, licking, and sucking the parts of your partner's body that bring you into a state of arousal.

---

[5] Bouchard, G., & Gallant, J. (2024). Differential effects of a brief body scan session on pain and anxiety levels. *Counselling and Psychotherapy Research, 24*, 1069–1075. https://doi.org/10.1002/capr.12785.

- **Focus on What You Can Smell:** What smells turn you on? Your partner's hair? Genitals? Lube? Focus on the smell of sex, arousal, pleasure, and joy.

Reconnection

This journey is about returning to yourself.

- Reconnect with your purpose
- Reconnect with your sexuality
- Reconnect with your inner voice, not society's noise

After intimacy, take a moment to reflect on the experience. Reflection is not about critiquing or over analyzing but about appreciating the connection, pleasure, and vulnerability shared. Ask yourself:

- What felt good about the experience, both emotionally and physically?
- How did being present and intentional change the way you felt about yourself and your partner?
- What did you learn about your own desires or your partner's?

This is also a time to show gratitude—to yourself for staying present and to your partner for sharing this intimate moment.[6] A simple verbal acknowledgment like, "I really enjoyed being close with you," or a silent reflection on the connection you've built can foster deeper intimacy.

By following the Mister Method for Mindful Sex, you can transform your sexual experiences. This method helps you stay present, reduces

---

[6] Diniz, G., Korkes, L., Tristão, L. S., Pelegrini, R., Bellodi, P. L., & Bernardo, W. M. (2023). The effects of gratitude interventions: A systematic review and meta-analysis. *Einstein (São Paulo), 21*, eRW0371. https://doi.org/10.31744/einstein_journal/2023RW0371

anxiety, and enhances your connection with your partner, leading to more fulfilling and enjoyable sex.[7]

COMMUNICATION MATTERS

The other piece of focusing on pleasure is increased communication about what you like, what your partner likes, and what sex acts are on the table (or floor, or bed . . .).

In Partnered Sex

We detail more about how to communicate with your partner in later chapters, but here's an overview.

- Open Communication: Start by discussing your desires, fears, and boundaries openly with your partner. This kind of transparency can build trust and deepen your connection.
- Express Emotions: Allow yourself to express emotions during sex—whether it's joy, love, or even moments of insecurity. Showing your emotional side can make the experience more intimate and authentic.
- Ask for What You Need: Being vulnerable means not only sharing your thoughts but also asking for what you emotionally and physically need during sex, which can lead to more fulfilling sexual experiences.
- Share Fantasies: Open up about your fantasies or sexual curiosities. This can be exciting and reveal deeper desires and aspects of your personality, enhancing your sexual bond.

---

[7] Hofmann, S. G., Sawyer, A. T., Witt, A. A., & Oh, D. (2010). The effect of mindfulness-based therapy on anxiety and depression: A meta-analytic review. *Journal of Consulting and Clinical Psychology, 78*(2), 169–183. https://doi.org/10.1037/a0018555.

- Post-Sex Discussion: Spend time after sex discussing what you enjoyed or what you might want to try differently next time. These conversations can improve your sexual experiences and ensure ongoing communication.

In Solo Sex

Yes, you have to communicate with yourself about sexual needs and preferences.

- Reflect on Your Desires: Use solo sex as a time to explore your own body and desires without judgment. Understanding your own needs and vulnerabilities can make you more confident and open in partnered situations.
- Mindful Masturbation: Focus on the sensations and emotions that arise during masturbation. Acknowledge any feelings of loneliness, anxiety, or pleasure without judgment to foster a deeper understanding of yourself.
- Journaling Post-Solo Sex: Write down thoughts and feelings post-masturbation. Reflecting on these experiences can help you understand your emotional responses and how they impact your sexual life.

LEAN INTO PLEASURE

For the third part in our four-part framework, it's important to know how to lean into pleasure. Ironically, when I suggest this, almost all of the guys I work with become immediately uncomfortable. After asking them what's wrong and doing some gentle probing, they tell me:

- That's being selfish, I should be focused on my partner's pleasure. If I focus on my pleasure, what will my partner think?

- I don't know how, sex feels good, what else is there? *(Tip: Learn to concentrate on different aspects of your body. As you get an erection, how do you know, what does it feel like? Lay down, be with your fantasy, how does your body feel, what is your breathing like? How does your penis feel? When you look down, how does it feel to see your erection? Can you move your penis without touching it?)*

Solo Sex Tips

Mindful masturbation allows you to show up for yourself, for the fantasy and imaginative part of you, engage your creativity, enjoy the moment, pleasure, etc.

Next time you masturbate, decide what you want to enjoy about the experience (set an intention). Then, during your masturbation session, focus on that one sensation.

What is the one thing you want to enjoy?

You might focus on:

- The feeling of pressure on your penis
- A different part of your body (your testicles, how they feel, your nipples, your butt)
- Pay attention to your breathing, how does it change?
- See list of erogenous zones in chapter 9

Partnered Sex

- Explore Sensory Play: Incorporate different sensations such as touch, taste, and sound. Use blindfolds, feathers, or different textures to enhance sensory stimulation.
- Experiment with Positions and Rhythms: Trying new positions and changing rhythms can help find what feels best, adding variety and excitement to the sexual experience.

- Practice Mutual Masturbation: Watching and being watched can be incredibly intimate and arousing, helping partners learn about each other's bodies and pleasure points.

GET OUT OF LOGISTICS

You don't need a map or a scene set up. The final component to the Mister Method, is, ironically, to ditch all maps (every one but *this* one). You don't need to be logistical about sex. You aren't mailing a package to family members overseas two weeks before Christmas. Sex is supposed to be fun and playful.

In response to this, my clients say:

- That's not the way my brain works.
- That's not how I run the rest of my life.
- That doesn't work for me.
- If there's no map I'll just lay on the bed and do nothing, I won't know what to do.
- If I don't plan, my partner won't have a good time.
- I'll come off as not being confident, I'll be unsure.
- If there's no plan, I'm afraid I'll fail.

When I hear these objections, I often say, I want to follow those thoughts. When I met with Steve, and discussed his fear of throwing out the flowchart he said:

"I worry I'll just wind up flopping on the bed like a fish."

"Let's follow that thought," I said, "Talk to me about flopping around like a fish on the bed, then what will happen?"

"I'll look like I don't know what I'm doing," Steve said, and then more came tumbling out, "I'll freeze, I'll do something wrong."

Other men have said that without the flowchart they fear they'll do something their partner won't like or fear their partner will respond terribly and decide to end the sexual encounter.

I remind them that this is where we talk about communication; it's okay to talk about sex before we have sex. In fact, in homosexual relationships, talking about sex before sex happens is vital because there isn't a penis-in-vagina flowchart. When both partners have the same parts, a discussion about what you're into, what's on the table and what isn't has to take place.

I dive into this conversation stuff in chapter 11 when we discuss partnered sex communication.

You can get out of your head, enjoy sex, and have the sex life you always hoped for.

After working on these four steps, Steve and his partner reported feeling more connected. They knew things would be uncomfortable along the way but committed to putting in the work for the sake of their relationship.

The couple worked on slowing down, prioritizing patience, and enjoying each other's company for as long as possible over pleasure or the euphoria from orgasms. Steve took the first step with vulnerability, opening up about his likes and fantasies. This paved the way for his partner to start talking about his fears and insecurities and made it possible for them to communicate openly about their sex life.

Though it was initially challenging, he eventually learned to appreciate leaning into pleasure, both in and out of his relationship. And finally, he put away every map but the mindfulness one laid out in this chapter, learning to stay in the moment and out of his head.

Nowadays, Steve feels at ease and confident. Since they started exploring it, the couple feels the seamless integration of pleasure and connection. Steve now understands what his partner was trying to say about "I want to feel more connected to you."

When you get out of your head, solo sex is more fun too. After several months, Matt was able to find relief from the erection issues and premature ejaculation during masturbation. He now has a variety of ways he enjoys masturbating—in the shower, in his bed, and on the couch—for starters.

He feels less shame about masturbation and no longer says, "I masturbate too much." He feels validated and normalized. Now, he knows that masturbation is a normal part of his sexuality and that he shouldn't feel shame about enjoying his own body.

CHAPTER TAKEAWAYS

- You will be able to be more connected to yourself and your partner if you manage to get out of your head.
- You will find yourself feeling more relaxed during sex and otherwise. (Practice mindfulness and meditation even when you aren't engaged sexually.)
- You'll learn to experience pleasure in a different way using the Mister Method.

CHAPTER 2

ARE MY SEXUAL FANTASIES NORMAL?

Let's take a minute to stroll down memory lane. Remember back to when you were a kid full of creativity and imagination. How did you pretend play when you were a kid? Think about all the things your young mind would create when you played. Did you play war with your army guys or play house or Barbies with your sisters? How did that go? Your army guys were in an epic battle shooting each other down because they had to fight to protect their territory from the enemy. You played the funny or nice or mean dad when your sister made you play house or dolls with her? Or perhaps you played cops and robbers where you were the meanest, baddest bad guy there ever was. You were shooting up the town, robbing banks, and stealing getaway cars right? Now, do you do those things as an adult? Are you out there masking up robbing banks and stealing getaway cars with your friends? Of course not. I mean I hope not. You might be reading the wrong book if those are your hobbies.

When I hear my daughter pretend playing, she is absolutely ruthless. She is mean and bossy and there is only one way to do things and that is her way. If you are playing with her she literally creates the script for you and is not afraid to call you out if you say it wrong. "No, you can't say that, you have to say blah blah . . ." She tells you exactly what you have to say. Or, "No, don't do it that way, you are playing wrong." Excuse my French, but she's a bitch in her pretend life. And honestly, I don't think I would really like her in real life. I'd be scared of her. At 4, 5, 6 years old her imagination seems to take her into the role of a 35-year-old

CEO boss bitch of her company bossing everyone around. Now, does that mean this is how she is always? No, not at all. She is actually a sweet little girl who follows the rules and hardly ever gets in trouble in real life. But in her pretend play she is the boss and nobody else has a chance. She wants to exert power and control and be bossy in her play, but that doesn't mean that's who she really is.

As we get older, our imagination doesn't disappear, it naturally takes different routes. When we start growing out of adolescence, we aren't so interested in toys and child play anymore and when we get to the teen years, our hormones are certainly making sure we think about more grown-up stuff, like sex in particular. It's what happens to all of us, right? There's nothing unnatural or wrong about it. As we grow up and start to sexually develop, our imagination and fantasies become sexual in nature. All the parts of our sexuality are brought to the table. That same playful imagination is at work, only now it's spiced up with sexuality.

My point is, fantasy, akin to imagination, is our mental playground where we can safely explore different parts of ourselves without the real-world consequences. It doesn't matter how old we are, it's our mind's way of trying on different roles, scenarios, and experiences. But just because you fantasize about something doesn't mean you actually want it to happen in real life.

I'm sure you have heard the common misconception that the sexual fantasies you have are things you want to do in real life. I want to be clear—that's wrong. What we imagine ourselves doing to someone, or what we imagine other people doing to us in the bedroom is a normal, healthy part of using the imagination/fantasy part of our brain. And yes, that often elicits a sexual response, right? An arousal response that feels good. Where I think we get tripped up here is in thinking that if we fantasize about being sexually dominated by someone, for example, then we must want to act that out in real life. But that's not always the case.

Our brains are wired for story and fantasy.[8] You might fantasize about leaving your job and moving to an island, or you might fantasize about what life would be like if you'd taken the high-powered career track instead of settling down in the suburbs and having kids. Fantasy is normal, some of those fantasies are sexual, but just because you fantasize about something doesn't mean you're about to leave your bungalow full of kids for a high-rise apartment. Sexual fantasy is simply a part of being an adult. We all have fantasies, and we all think differently about them. The important thing to know is that it is completely normal. All of it, even if it feels wild or off the wall, and there is nothing to feel ashamed about. Fantasy certainly can be the gateway to exploring other things that you might be interested in. But sometimes fantasy is just that, fantasy.

FANTASIES MEN HAVE

Let's take a dive into a common fantasy I see from multiple men who come into my office: Watching their partner have sex with someone else. Many men say they like imagining that scene, it's really arousing to think of, and that they could definitely use that scene to masturbate to and have a great experience, but in reality, they would never be able to handle that. One of my clients, Brad, said, "It is really hot to think about hyper focusing on my wife's pleasure while being fucked by another man, but if that really happened, if she came to me and said, 'Hey honey I really wanna have sex with another man,' I'd be destroyed."

When he said that, I immediately knew what to ask next. I said, "Brad, do you watch her while you are having sex with her?"

---

[8] Dill-Shackleford, K. E., Vinney, C., & Hopper-Losenicky, K. (2016). Connecting the dots between fantasy and reality: The social psychology of our engagement with fictional narrative and its functional value. *Social and Personality Psychology Compass, 10*(11), 634–646. https://doi.org/10.1111/spc3.12274.

"No," he answered, looking a little puzzled. There it is, he's too busy being in his own head during sex. So I told him, "You realize that is possible, right? You are always talking about how you are always multitasking, well here's an opportunity for you to multitask, just a little differently. You can hyperfocus on her pleasure while you fuck her or you could even watch her pleasure herself, with consent of course." It was like a light bulb had switched on for him. Brad suddenly realized he can watch her enjoy herself with him or maybe even when she pleasures herself and he can still get the enjoyment he felt from the fantasy without acting out anything he's not comfortable with in real life.

See that's the beauty of fantasy. We don't have to actually do the things that excite us to imagine. We can do all of it, none of it, or we could take parts of it and leave the rest in our imagination. It's up to you and your partner how far you go.

Some men get aroused at the thought of public nudity, but they aren't running to their nearest Walmart to compare bananas (please don't do that). Some men fantasize about having sex in public, but that's all it is, a fantasy, an internal image to use for pleasure. It's fun to fantasize about being bad, about the shock factor such behavior would have on the people around us, but the majority of us can be taken out in public and behave ourselves.

I made a list of some of the common fantasies men have. I want you to read them and see how they make you feel.

- Watching their partner have sex with someone else
- Domination (both ways)
- Transgender people
- Orgies
- Lesbian sex
- Threesomes
- Same-sex fantasies
- Power play (dom/sub relationships)
- Anonymous sex
- Sex workers

Although common, sometimes some of the spicy fantasies we have don't sit well with us. Something about fantasizing about having anal sex or having sex with someone other than our partner tugs at our moral compass. For whatever reason, we feel shame for thinking what we are thinking. This brings us to exploring feeling shame from our fantasies.

WHEN FANTASY BRINGS SHAME

I will never forget, fifteen years or so ago, I worked with a war veteran, I'll call him Adam. He walked into my office extremely dysregulated. He felt suicidal because he had been watching porn he morally didn't agree with. Adam had come across rape porn and he found it to be really arousing. He wasn't sure why and in fact, the scenes took his mind back to combat where he had witnessed multiple rapes of women in the village. It triggered his PTSD and made him feel deep shame he didn't know what to do with. He told me with deep anguish, "I am a horrible person who should now be categorized as a rapist because I get aroused by rape porn."

During our sessions, we broke it all down. Adam was already aroused and engaged when he watched porn. That's the intent of porn, right? It's intended to hook you in, similar to Netflix, it's a form of media after all. It wants you engaged and aroused, otherwise what's the point? He was aroused by the content, he was aroused by the woman in the scene, and he was aroused by the act of penetration. He was aroused by all the other pieces. The rape aspect of the film is something he identified as being morally wrong. He would never rape anyone in real life. In fact, during his time in the village, he chose not to rape the women when so many others did.

Once we peeled the situation down to its core, Adam felt a huge sense of relief. He was able to understand that being aroused by a scene in a porn film doesn't mean he must want to do that himself and that he must belong within a subsection of people.

When men come to me to talk about their sexual fantasies, it's usually because they are feeling shame about something they fantasize about. Something about the fantasies they have is fighting with their core beliefs. It's not sitting well with them, and they can't handle feeling the shame any longer.

Shame from sexual fantasies can stem from societal "norms" you've been led to believe as absolute truth and tried hard to abide by. Or the shame could be from something more personal, like the judgment of a past partner, or from the fear of what family or friends would think if they knew what you thought about. These are what we call core beliefs, strong, long-term beliefs we have that help us understand how the world works and who we are. I want to share some of the core beliefs I have found that bring men shame around sexual fantasies:

- I am married and shouldn't fantasize about other people. If I fantasize about other people, I'm not a good husband, partner, etc. I'm flawed, and potentially, I might not want to stay in this marriage.
- My partner owns my sexuality—I have to give it to them for the relationship to work.
- You shouldn't have to masturbate; your partner should meet all your needs. If you have fantasies outside of marriage, there must be something wrong with you or with your partner.
- If I'm thinking about it and fantasizing about it, it means I want to do it.
- I don't think my fantasy is morally sound, so I worry about what this means about me as a person.
- If anyone else found out about this, they'd leave me. I'd have no friends or family.
- In a monogamous relationship, you only need your partner, and your partner will meet all your needs.

There is an endless number of fantasies men have that bring them shame because they don't exactly equate them with the person they are and that can be confusing. Perhaps you can relate to one or more of these common core beliefs leading to shame. If so, don't worry. You are not alone and I will help you sort it out.

ACCEPTABLE VS. UNACCEPTABLE FANTASIES

You wouldn't believe how many men tell me they avoid the beach because they don't want to even have the opportunity to look at other human bodies for fear of the potential outcome. One of my clients actually told me, "I avoid the beach. I won't even go with my wife because it's a recipe for getting in trouble." He runs with the thought that if his wife saw him looking at other women in bikinis she would get pissed and automatically assume he is thinking about fucking them.

The beach is a good example because there are a number of different reasons we avoid going. Sometimes it's hard to tell how old people are, right? And we damn sure don't want to get in that kind of mess. We usually don't want to come off as a creepy old dude staring at half-naked people on the beach either. What is the baseline anyway, between looking and staring? Is it one second, or is it three seconds? There is no way to answer that so avoidance is the easiest, safest route. We typically don't aim to make other people feel uncomfortable. And the fact is, a lot of men don't trust themselves to stop whatever goes on in their minds, so they simply don't let it start.

ACTIONABLE STEPS TO WORK THROUGH SHAME

If I have done my job well, then now you have a better understanding of what fantasy really is. Now it is up to you what you decide to do with them. It's a personal adventure, there's no cookie cutter for these cookies and it's not something I can Men's-Sex-Health-Expert out for you. I can't sit here and tell you that checking out a person for three seconds is okay . . . you have to come up with your own boundaries. It's up to you what is acceptable for you to do in relation to your fantasy with the goal of exterminating the shame.

You don't have to hold on to or bury the shame you feel from your sexual fantasies. Actually, please don't do that. I have some tried and true action steps for you to work through those feelings. Take a look:

- Recognizing when shame creeps in. Take a dive within and dig a little bit to figure out where the shame is coming from. Is it because you've had it drilled in your head by what society deems acceptable? Have you told your partner your fantasies and they reacted or said something negative about you? Is it because your religious beliefs are strict on sex stuff and what you fantasize about is seen as unacceptable to your religion? Or perhaps it's past experiences where things took a wrong turn for you?
- Exert your power and control. You don't have to let society, your partner, your church, or anyone else dictate your core beliefs regarding your fantasies. You get to decide what feels right to you. If you say looking at a sexy person for three seconds is okay, but then you sit in shame once you do it, then it's not okay to you.
- Collect skills and strategies to heal the parts that cause the shameful feeling.
    - Use self-talk and say something to yourself like, "I find that person attractive. I am going to admire them for that and let it stop there. It's okay to notice attractive people."

- Separate fantasy from reality by reminding yourself what is happening in the moment, in real life. For example, if you are fantasizing about something you think is morally wrong, remind yourself, "This is my imagination, it's not real. I am not actually doing this, nor will I, but I am willing to let myself imagine what it would be like for the purpose of letting go." Never forget that fantasy is part of being a healthy human being.
- Give yourself reminders. I find it works pretty well if I leave myself notes in a private place to look back on if I start to feel a certain way about what happens in my head.
  - Fantasy is a healthy part of sexuality.
  - My fantasies do not define my morality.
  - Communicate with my partner.
  - I have control over my fantasies.
  - I have control over my actions.
- Talk to a therapist if you feel like you are trying everything but still fight with the shame.

When you have a fantasy you want to explore in real life, you have to first acknowledge it and think about what you should do if you want to explore it. What steps are necessary to bring this fantasy to reality? If you are in a relationship, I highly recommend communicating your fantasies with your partner—it's a must if they involve them. If you're having solo sex fantasies you can keep them to yourself if you wish. That's okay, too. You only have to invite them into masturbation time if you want to. I do invite you to try inviting them into solo sex time because that can be really fun for you both.

Because many of us learn better with visuals, I have put together this flow chart for exploring your fantasies.

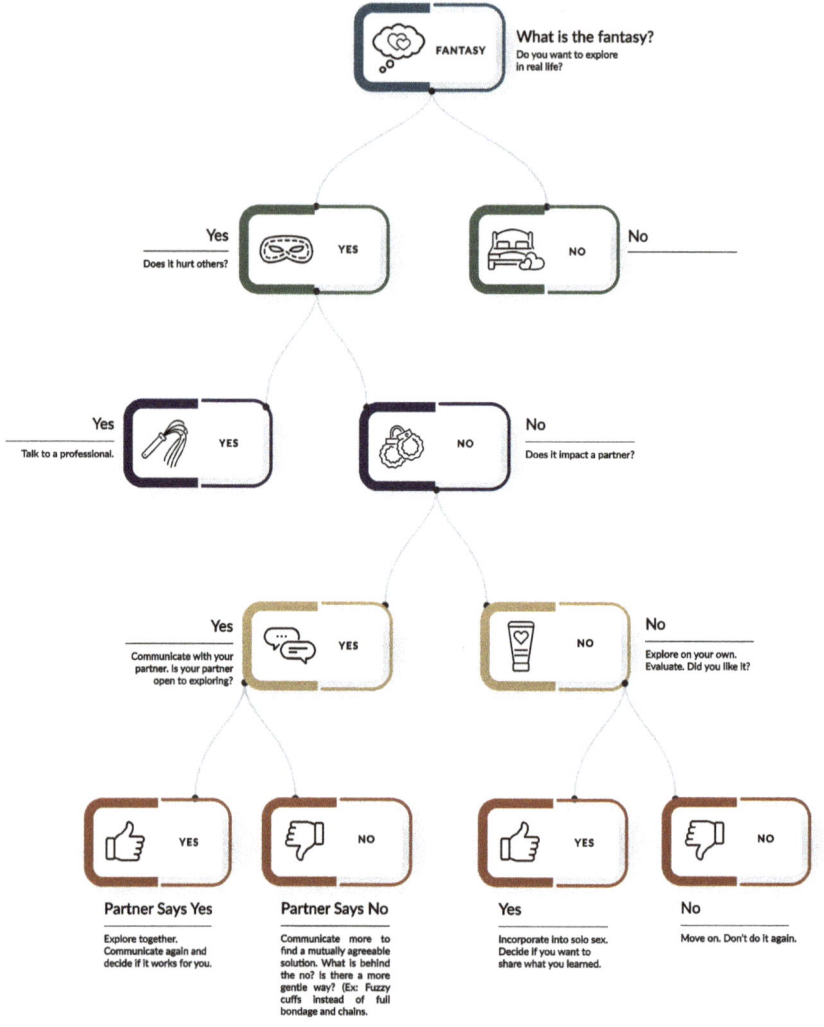

It's important to remember that if your partner says no to exploring a fantasy with you, you have to respect that. That's not to say that you can't talk about it more and come up with something you would both be willing to try. Maybe they don't want to fully commit to dom/sub play but may be willing to try fuzzy handcuffs. Like any other aspect of a relationship, there's a little give and a little take for both of you.

Along those same lines, you may find that you or your partner don't even like doing something after trying it. That's okay, too. Communicate with your partner every step of the way and see where each other's fantasies take you.

Fantasy, the playground of our mind, is where we live out our wildest adventures without leaving our living room. It's normal and perfectly fine to have fantasies that seem a little out there because, remember, it's a fantasy, and having it doesn't mean you want to make it a reality. Fantasy is our safe space where our imagination is free to run wild, exploring different aspects of our desires without the baggage of real-world consequences. If you ever feel shame and need to discuss them, know that you are not alone. It's all natural to being a human. Give yourself freedom to enjoy your fantasy and to seek help when you need it.

CHAPTER TAKEAWAYS

- Sexual fantasies are a natural and healthy part of human sexuality.
- Fantasizing about something does not mean acting on it in real life.
- Exploring fantasies without shame allows for deeper self-discovery and intimacy.

CHAPTER 3

IS IT OKAY TO LIKE THIS? UNDERSTANDING KINKS AND BDSM

"Why is it that I can so enjoy flogging my wife when I love her so much?"

A client who enjoyed BDSM with his wife asked during a session one day. I knew immediately that he was experiencing some cognitive dissonance over the seemingly polarizing ideas that he could enjoy flogging his wife while also calling her the love of his life.

"I mean, she consented to the flogging. Really, the whole BDSM thing was her idea at first. But now, I don't know, I love it. What does that mean about me?"

DEFINING BDSM AND KINK

BDSM stands for Bondage, Discipline, Dominance, Submission, Sadism, and Masochism. It encompasses a variety of activities that involve power exchange, restraint, and sensory play. Kink, on the other hand, is a broader term that refers to any sexual interest or activity outside of what is considered "vanilla" sex. Kinks can range from role-playing to fetishes, and BDSM is one category within kink.

In a 2020 study published in the *Journal of Sex Research* nearly 40% to 70% of people surveyed reported fantasizing about BDSM activities, and another 20% regularly engaged in them. There are a plethora of ways to engage in BDSM, both solo and partnered.[9] Here is a non-exhaustive list.

- Sexual sensation play involves playing with feathers, scarves, massage oils, spanking, nipple clamps or sensory deprivation using blindfolds or ear plugs.
- Temperature play involves using warm, cold, icy, or hot things like metal, jewelry, wax, and ice to heighten sensations.
- Impact play is when partners strike one another using hands, paddles, whips, floggers, and other items.
- Breath control play or erotic asphyxiation is intentionally restricting oxygen during sexual play. It's important to note that breath control play can cause accidental death.
- Restraint play involves restricting movement in some way during sexual activity. This could be with rope, cuffs, silk scarves, or just your hand.

THE LINK BETWEEN BDSM AND INTIMACY

Now that we have a definition, let's go back to my client's question. How could he enjoy hitting his wife during their BDSM sessions when he loved her so much? Many people find that BDSM fosters deep intimacy and trust between partners.[10] The negotiation, communication, and vulnerability required for BDSM experiences often strengthen relationships and enhance sexual satisfaction.

In addition, I've found in my work with clients that, for most people, the intense dom/sub relationship that exists in their sexual play doesn't

---

[9] Brown, A., Barker, E. D., & Rahman, Q. (2020). A systematic scoping review of the prevalence, etiological, psychological, and interpersonal factors associated with BDSM. *The Journal of Sex Research, 57*(6), 781–811. https://doi.org/10.1080/00224499.2019.1665619.

[10] Rogak, H., & Connor, J. (2017). Practice of consensual BDSM and relationship satisfaction. *Sexual and Relationship Therapy, 33*(1), 1–16. https://doi.org/10.1080/14681994.2017.1419560.

leave the bedroom. So, of course my client can love his wife and still flog her when she asks. To explore this further, let's look at my Autonomous Sexuality Model.

THE AUTONOMOUS SEXUALITY MODEL

The Autonomous Sexuality Model I discussed in Chapter 3 emphasizes that individuals have the right to explore and define their own sexual preferences. Whether BDSM and kink fit into your sexual identity is entirely up to you. Some people find these experiences thrilling and fulfilling, while others may not enjoy them after trying. Both are completely valid perspectives.

EXPLORATION WITHOUT PRESSURE

It's okay to be interested in something conceptually but realize it's not for you in practice. I have a friend who visited a BDSM club because they were curious and then decided anything beyond light impact play is definitely not for them. The key is to lean into curiosity and give yourself permission to explore what excites you. There are many ways to incorporate BDSM into your sex life, and it exists on a wide intensity spectrum—some activities don't involve penetrative sex at all, which can be appealing for those focused on power dynamics, sensation play, or emotional intimacy.

CORNERSTONES OF BDSM

Engaging in BDSM involves a power exchange, which makes safety, consent, and communication fundamental to a fulfilling and risk-aware experience. Whether you are new to BDSM or a seasoned practitioner, taking the time to establish clear boundaries, prioritize well-being, and practice aftercare ensures a positive and empowering experience.

CONSENT

Consent in BDSM goes beyond a simple "yes" or "no." It must be enthusiastic, informed, specific, and ongoing. Consent should be:

- Negotiated in advance: Discuss limits, desires, boundaries, and triggers before engaging in play.
- Mutual and freely given: Both (or all) participants must be comfortable and enthusiastic about the activity.
- Revocable at any time: A person can withdraw consent at any moment, and the play must stop immediately.

Types of Consent:

- Affirmative Consent: Both parties explicitly agree to participate in specific activities.
- Informed Consent: Everyone understands the risks involved before proceeding.
- Ongoing Consent: Consent is not a one-time agreement. Check in throughout the experience.

SETTING UP THE SCENE: PLANNING FOR SAFETY

A well-planned BDSM scene ensures that all participants feel physically and emotionally safe. Consider these factors:
Discuss Hard and Soft Limits:

- Hard limits are nonnegotiable boundaries (e.g., no blood play or humiliation).
- Soft limits are activities that might be okay under certain conditions (e.g., spanking only with a certain level of intensity).

Establish Safe Words and Signals:

- A safe word (like "red") immediately stops the scene.
- A caution word (like "yellow") signals a need to slow down or check in.
- Nonverbal signals (such as dropping an object or tapping out) are important in situations where verbal communication isn't possible.

If a partner disregards a safe word or pushes limits without consent, it is a violation of trust and should be addressed seriously.

Choose a Safe Location: If engaging in BDSM for the first time, a private and controlled environment is best.

Have Emergency Protocols: If bondage or intense play is involved, always have safety scissors, first-aid supplies, and a backup plan.

AFTERCARE: PHYSICAL AND EMOTIONAL RECOVERY

Aftercare is the emotional and physical support provided after a BDSM scene. The intensity of some activities can lead to drop—a sudden emotional low due to endorphin and adrenaline depletion. Some aftercare strategies include:

- Physical care: Hydration, cuddling, massages, or using blankets.
- Emotional reassurance: Talking about feelings, affirming consent and mutual care, and decompressing.
- Time to process: Some people need alone time, while others benefit from immediate comfort.
- Check-ins the next day: Emotional responses can surface later, so follow up after a session.

COMMUNITY AND EDUCATION: LEARNING FROM OTHERS

Many BDSM practitioners find support, mentorship, and education in local and online communities. Many of my clients enjoy connecting with others on FetLife, a social media site for folks who want to explore new avenues of sexuality. Others don't like the overt sexual vibe of that site. I'd encourage you to look for local meetups of folks into BDSM, or even find a BDSM club to help you build community. Engaging with the community helps with:

- Learning best practices: Workshops, books, and discussions can provide valuable insights.
- Finding vetted partners: Trusted communities help screen potential play partners.
- Reducing stigma: Being part of a group that understands BDSM dynamics can create a safe space for discussion.

Full disclosure, I debated for a long time about where to put information about BDSM in this book. I wanted to mention it explicitly, so I considered sprinkling it throughout the book, but it's such an important part of sexual lives for many people I felt it warranted its own chapter. Then, I worried that putting the information in one chapter would make the BDSM community feel as if they didn't belong in the other chapters.

Ultimately, I set this chapter apart because I want any person who picks up this book and is curious about BDSM to know they are getting a dose of info in these pages. However, I want to explicitly state that the rest of this book, everything from the next chapter on porn to the chapters on communication and sexual challenges are all for the BDSM community as well as those who don't practice BDSM.

CHAPTER TAKEAWAYS

- BDSM and kink are more common than you think. BDSM, which includes Bondage, Discipline, Dominance, Submission, Sadism, and Masochism, is just one part of a broad spectrum of kinks. Kink is simply any sexual interest beyond "vanilla" sex, and it exists on a wide spectrum—from light sensory play to power dynamics and impact play.
- BDSM can strengthen intimacy and trust. Engaging in BDSM requires deep levels of communication, trust, and negotiation, which often lead to stronger relationships. The emotional and psychological aspects of BDSM do not contradict love or affection; rather, they can enhance intimacy by creating shared experiences of vulnerability and pleasure. The Autonomous Sexuality Model affirms that sexual exploration should be free from shame and guided by personal autonomy.
- Consent, safety, and communication are essential. In BDSM, consent is more than a simple "yes" or "no"—it must be negotiated in advance, freely given, and revocable at any time. Establishing safe words and nonverbal signals, setting clear boundaries (hard and soft limits), and having emergency protocols are critical for ensuring a positive experience. Consent violations are serious breaches of trust and must be addressed immediately.
- Aftercare and community support enhance the experience. Aftercare is the emotional and physical support following a BDSM scene, helping partners process intense experiences and recover from endorphin drops. Additionally, connecting with the BDSM community—whether online or in local groups—can provide education, mentorship, and a safe space to explore kink with informed guidance.

CHAPTER 4

WHAT'S THE DEAL WITH PORN?

In the previous chapters we discussed that fantasies are a normal part of sexuality, just like daydreaming about an ideal vacation or an alternate career path. Porn is sexual fantasy in HD, and, like your social media feed, it's designed to capture and hold your attention. At its most basic level, porn is just media; but, because it's sexually explicit media, people have a lot to say about it.

UNDERSTANDING PORNOGRAPHY

Education and open dialogue are crucial in addressing the complexities of pornography, as they provide the foundation for a more informed and nuanced understanding of its various impacts. By fostering awareness and facilitating conversations, we can better navigate the multifaceted issues surrounding pornography, from its psychological and behavioral effects to its social and ethical implications. In that effort, let's explore some common questions that arise when discussing pornography. This exploration aims to equip everyone with the knowledge to engage in thoughtful and constructive discourse.

It's important to note, there is so much disagreement in the porn addiction community around these claims. You will find journal articles who support this and others who dispute it. My goal here is to help you understand how porn use impacts you, and ways you can reduce maladaptive thinking and behavior patterns so you can enjoy a healthier relationship with your sexuality.

WHAT DOES PORN USE REVEAL ABOUT A RELATIONSHIP?

Porn use in a relationship can reveal various aspects, depending on the individuals involved. It might indicate a healthy sexual curiosity and exploration, or it could point to underlying issues such as unmet sexual needs. Open and honest communication about porn use is crucial to understanding each other's motivations and maintaining a healthy relationship dynamic.

DOES PORNOGRAPHY USE CAUSE ERECTILE DYSFUNCTION?

There is no direct cause-and-effect relationship. It is possible that excessive pornography use can contribute to erectile dysfunction (ED) in some individuals. This condition, sometimes referred to as porn-induced erectile dysfunction (PIED), occurs when a person becomes so accustomed to the specific type of arousal provided by porn that they find it difficult to achieve or maintain an erection during real life sexual encounters. For others, porn may be used to enhance sexual activity.

HOW MANY PEOPLE WATCH PORN?

A significant portion of the population watches porn. A 2022 survey in *Sexuality Research and Social Policy* suggests that over 85% of people have used porn, with men showing higher rates of self-reported use than women.[11] While exact numbers can vary, it is clear that porn

---

[11] Ballester-Arnal, R., García-Barba, M., Castro-Calvo, J., Gómez, C., Gil-Llario, M. D., & Gil-Juliá, B. (2023). Pornography consumption in people of different age groups: An analysis based on gender, contents, and consequences. *Sexuality Research and Social Policy, 20*(4), 766–779. https://doi.org/10.1007/s13178-022-00720-z.

consumption is a common activity across various demographics. And, with the rise of social media, sites like OnlyFans, and AI sex chats, what people define as porn is changing.[12]

CHANGES IN PORN PREFERENCES

Over time, some individuals notice shifts in their porn preferences, a phenomenon known as porn escalation. This occurs when someone requires increasingly intense content to maintain the same level of excitement. Self-assessment and reflection can help determine whether these changes are driven by genuine interest or by habit. Asking questions like, "Am I watching this because I enjoy it, or because it's what I've become accustomed to?" can provide valuable insight.

SHAME AND GUILT

Shame and guilt about porn use often stem from cultural, societal, or personal values. Addressing these emotions involves understanding their origins. Are they based on personal beliefs, or have they been internalized from external sources? Cognitive behavioral techniques, mindfulness, and self-compassion can help individuals move beyond shame and develop a more balanced view of their sexuality.

COGNITIVE BEHAVIORAL TECHNIQUES (CBT)

Harsh self-judgment often accompanies porn use. Thoughts like, "I'm a terrible person for watching this" or "I should be able to control myself"

---

[12] Wright, P. J., Tokunaga, R., & Herbenick, D. (2023). But do porn sites get more traffic than TikTok, OpenAI, and Zoom? *The Journal of Sex Research*, *60*(6), 763–767. https://doi.org/10.1080/00224499.2023.2186762.

can lead to shame and avoidance rather than positive change. Cognitive Behavioral Therapy (CBT) helps challenge these negative thoughts and replaces them with more balanced perspectives.

For example, instead of, "I'm weak for watching porn," a CBT-based reframe might be, "I'm learning about my triggers and working on my relationship with porn." Self-compassion and mindfulness further support this process by helping individuals observe their thoughts without judgment and develop a healthier relationship with their sexuality.

DISTINGUISHING BETWEEN PORN, FANTASY, AND MASTURBATION

Many people often lump porn, fantasy, and masturbation together as if they are the same thing. They are not. They are distinct experiences.

Fantasy

Fantasy involves using your imagination to create arousing scenarios in your mind. It can be about anything that excites you and doesn't require any external media.

Porn

Porn is external content designed to stimulate sexual arousal. It can include videos, images, stories, or audio and can serve as an aid for arousal or as a way to explore fantasies.

Masturbation

Masturbation is the physical act of self-pleasure. It can be done with or without the aid of porn or fantasy. While porn can be a helpful tool for masturbation, it is not a necessity.

Trying Masturbation Without Porn

I meet many men who can only masturbate with porn. Over time, this reliance made it difficult for them to enjoy the act without visual stimulation. To address this, they tried to masturbate using only their fantasy and imagination. This process helped them slow down, become more in tune with their body, and rediscover the pleasure of their own thoughts and feelings.

Sitting by yourself and using your imagination can enhance your self-awareness and provide a deeper, more personal experience. Separating these three aspects—fantasy, porn, and masturbation—helps you better understand your own desires and find balance in your sexual habits.

COULD I BE ADDICTED TO PORN?

Society talks about addiction all the time—whether it's cupcakes, social media, or video games. The term is often applied loosely. However, when it comes to sex or pornography, the conversation takes on a more serious tone. The first thing to recognize is that sex and porn are not substances—they are natural behaviors or forms of media. Trying to categorize them alongside drugs or alcohol can be misleading.

Terms like "porn addiction" or "sex addiction" are often used, yet neither is recognized in the DSM-5, the diagnostic manual used by mental health professionals. The DSM-5 specifically states, "At this time, there is insufficient peer-reviewed evidence to establish the diagnostic criteria and course descriptions needed to identify these behaviors as mental health disorders."[13]

So, what's really going on when someone struggles with porn use? Often, early exposure to porn is surrounded by secrecy, shame, and

---

[13] American Psychiatric Association. (2013). *Diagnostic and statistical manual of mental disorders* (5th ed.). https://doi.org/10.1176/appi.books.9780890425596.

confusion. This secrecy can lead to a rushed, habitual approach to porn and masturbation that carries into adulthood, shaping how individuals relate to their sexuality.

People use porn for various reasons, including:

- Sexual arousal
- Exploring fantasies
- Learning about sex
- Masturbating
- Disconnecting from daily stress
- Relieving stress, depression, or anxiety

All these reasons can be valid, but they can also become a problem depending on your intent and behavior. For instance, using porn as a form of education can be helpful if you are looking to spice things up or explore new positions or fantasies. At the same time, it can be tricky. Porn isn't filmed with the idea of education. While it might give you ideas about anal sex, it doesn't provide a comprehensive guide on how to engage in it safely and consensually with your partner.

The extent to which you rely on porn for these solutions can also be an issue. If porn is your only way to fantasize, achieve sexual satisfaction, masturbate, or learn about sex, it might indicate a problem. However, if it's just one of the tools you use occasionally, it can be part of a healthy lifestyle.

As we've already discussed, it's perfectly okay to use porn as a way to disconnect, just as some people might choose to read, binge-watch Netflix, or scroll through social media. These activities can serve as valuable tools for relaxation and stress relief, helping to provide a break from the demands of daily life. They allow you to unwind and recharge, which is essential to maintaining mental health.

However, it's essential to recognize that when any of these activities become your primary or sole means of disconnecting, it can indicate an underlying issue. For instance, spending excessive amounts of time on any one activity—such as reading for twelve hours straight, binge-watching an entire season of a show without breaks, or constantly seeking arousal through porn—might indicate that you're using these activities to avoid dealing with deeper problems or emotions.

Emotional Triggers and Coping Mechanisms

Some people use porn as a way to escape difficult emotions like stress, anxiety, or loneliness. Watching a video provides a quick dopamine hit, offering temporary relief without addressing the underlying emotional issue.

Healthy emotional regulation is key to breaking this cycle. It starts with recognizing triggers and understanding why you're watching porn. Once you have that awareness, you can explore alternative ways to manage emotions, such as taking a walk, practicing deep breathing, journaling, or talking to a trusted friend. These healthier habits help you regain control and reduce compulsive use.

Balance and moderation are key to ensuring that your habits remain healthy and beneficial. Here are a few tips to help maintain a balanced approach:

1. **Set Time Limits:** Allocate specific amounts of time for leisure activities. For example, limit yourself to an hour of TV or a certain number of chapters in a book before taking a break.
2. **Diversify Your Activities:** To disconnect, engage in a variety of activities. Mix reading with physical exercise, socializing with friends, or pursuing hobbies that don't involve screens or sexual content.
3. **Stay Mindful:** Be aware of why you're turning to these activities. Are you using them to genuinely relax, or are you trying to avoid something? Mindfulness can help you understand your motivations and make healthier choices.
4. **Monitor Impact on Life:** Keep an eye on how your chosen activities affect your daily responsibilities and relationships. If you notice negative impacts, it might be time to reassess and adjust your habits.

5. **Seek Healthy Coping Mechanisms:** If you find yourself relying heavily on porn, reading, or other activities to disconnect, explore other coping mechanisms like meditation, journaling, or talking to a friend or therapist.

Understanding when your leisure activities are becoming problematic is crucial. Signs that you might be over-relying on porn or other forms of entertainment include:

- Neglecting responsibilities at work, school, or home.
- Experiencing conflicts in your relationships due to your habits.
- Feeling distressed or anxious when you can't engage in these activities.
- Using these activities as a primary way to cope with stress or negative emotions.

HOW DOES PORN AFFECT MY BRAIN?

The actual truth is that this area of human sexuality research is so new, we don't have a lot of concrete answers. I know that can be frustrating when all you want is a clear direction that will lead to sexual satisfaction and healthy connection. There are a few researchers diving into the effects of pornography on the human brain and, so, since I'm not a researcher, I'll simply report what these sex-positive researchers have uncovered so far.

It is possible that pornography use can affect the brain.[14] Viewing porn triggers the release of dopamine, a neurotransmitter associated with pleasure and reward. Dopamine isn't bad for you, and, in fact, is often part of what motivates you to do things like go to the gym or finish the report for work. Over time, though, consistent exposure to porn can

---

[14] Prause, N., Steele, V. R., Staley, C., Sabatinelli, D., & Hajcak, G. (2015). Modulation of late positive potentials by sexual images in problem users and controls inconsistent with "porn addiction." *Biological Psychology, 109*, 192–199. https://doi.org/10.1016/j.biopsycho.2015.06.005.

lead to changes in the brain's reward system, potentially affecting your response to sexual stimuli and overall behavior.[15] Basically, if you watch "too much" porn you could stop responding to real life sexual experiences in the way you once did. However, the extent of these changes varies among individuals and depends on the frequency and nature of porn consumption. What is too much for you could be just fine for the person next to you.

Rather than using the label "addiction," a more useful term is **problematic porn use**, which focuses on the actual impact on a person's life. Signs of problematic porn use include:

- Watching more than intended
- Inability to reduce use despite wanting to
- Negative impact on relationships or daily responsibilities
- Feelings of distress or guilt after watching

If these apply to you, self-assessment, therapy, or support groups can be helpful next steps.

HOW CAN I SEEK HELP IF I THINK MY PORN USE IS PROBLEMATIC?

If you think you have a problem with porn, seeking help can involve several steps:

- **Self-Assessment:** Recognize and acknowledge the problem.
- **Professional Help:** Consult an American Association of Sexuality Educators, Counselors and Therapists (AASECT) certified

---

[15] Ince, C., Albertella, L., Liu, C., Tiego, J., Fontenelle, L. F., Chamberlain, S. R., Yücel, M., & Rotaru, K. (2024). Problematic pornography use and novel patterns of escalating use: A cross-sectional network analysis with two independent samples. *Addictive Behaviors, 156*, 108048. https://doi.org/10.1016/j.addbeh.2024.108048.

therapist or counselor specializing in sexual health or addiction. This is the certification I hold and will ensure you're working with a therapist who isn't afraid to take a deep dive into pornography conversations. Learn more here https://www.aasect.org/.
- **Support Groups:** Join support groups where you can share experiences and strategies with others facing similar issues.
- **Education:** Learn about addiction and its effects to better understand your situation.
- **Coaching:** Sexual health coaching is different from therapy. Coaching is more future-focused, guided by goal setting, and targeted to achieve your stated purpose. Just be sure the person you're working with is certified just as you'd want a therapist to be.

CAN I USE PORN RESPONSIBLY?

Rather than pathologize normal human sexual behavior, I prefer to talk about how to make values-based decisions about your sexuality. So, I put together a porn use guide to help you think about how, why, and when you use porn.

A responsible approach to porn use involves:

- **Self-Assessment:** Regularly evaluating whether porn is enhancing or interfering with your life.
- **Intent and Function:** Understanding why you use porn and whether that aligns with your values.
- **Balance and Moderation:** Engaging in a variety of sexual and non-sexual activities for fulfillment.
- **Communication:** Discussing porn use openly with partners to ensure mutual understanding and boundaries.
- **Seeking Help When Needed:** If porn use becomes distressing or unmanageable, seeking professional guidance can be beneficial.

Value-Based Decision-Making

Using the Autonomous Sexuality Model, you can make intentional, value-based decisions about porn use. This involves:

- **Time Management and Boundaries:** Setting limits on porn consumption to ensure it doesn't interfere with daily life.
- **Mindful Masturbation:** Engaging in self-pleasure with awareness and intention rather than as a rushed or shame-filled act.
- **Ethical Porn Consumption:** Choosing content that aligns with one's values, such as ensuring consent and fair treatment of performers.

Ethical vs. Unethical Porn	Ethical Porn	Unethical Porn
Consent	Explicit consent from all participants	Potential lack of or coerced consent
Fair Pay	Fair wages and profit-sharing	Low or no pay, exploitation
Representation	Diverse and realistic portrayals	Stereotypical, unrealistic depiction
Production Practices	Safe, consensual, and transparent	Unsafe, exploitative, or secretive
Respect for Participants	Focus on well-being and dignity	Disregard for rights and dignity

Making value-based decisions about the type and frequency of porn use can help reduce shame and promote a healthier, more intentional relationship with sexual media.

Pornography, designed to spark sexual arousal, comes in many forms and for a variety of purposes. Much like Netflix hooks its viewers, porn captivates audiences, often with the aim of maintaining our attention and selling advertisements. This content can range from erotic stories, images, and audio to explicit videos and more subtle forms like suggestive social media posts.

Pornography can include traditional mediums like Playboy, modern platforms like OnlyFans, and even AI chatbots. It's pervasive across various channels, including Twitter, Instagram, and Reddit, where seemingly innocuous posts—like images or videos of women in bathing suits—can also be considered erotic content by some.

Defining what constitutes pornography is highly subjective and can vary significantly from one person to another. This subjective nature means that it is crucial to discuss and agree upon these definitions in relationships. For instance, one partner might view OnlyFans as a form of pornographic content. At the same time, others might see engaging with an AI chatbot as a form of infidelity. These differing perceptions highlight the importance of clear communication to avoid misunderstandings and potential conflicts.

FINAL THOUGHTS

Pornography, like any form of media, can be a tool for exploration or a source of conflict, depending on how it's used. The key is intention, awareness, and balance. Rather than labeling all porn use as harmful or all-consuming, it's more helpful to explore how it functions in your life. Through self-reflection and value-based decision-making, individuals can develop a healthy and shame-free relationship with their sexuality.

For further guidance, consider exploring my Porn Addiction Reimagined Course for a deeper dive into mindful and intentional porn use.

CHAPTER TAKEAWAYS

In this chapter, we've explored various aspects of pornography use, its effects, and how to engage with it responsibly. Here are the key takeaways to help you maintain a balanced and healthy relationship with porn:

- Recognize that porn, fantasy, and masturbation are distinct but often interconnected aspects of sexual expression.
- Acknowledge that porn can affect the brain by altering its reward system, similar to other pleasurable activities.
- Responsible use guideline, moderation, communication with your partner, and seeking help if you find yourself plagued by shame, guilt, or stress related to porn use.
- Rather than talking about porn addiction, I prefer the term problematic porn use to describe porn use that impacts your life and mental health in negative ways.

CHAPTER 5

HOW MUCH MASTURBATION IS TOO MUCH?

In today's digital age, online searches can often lead to a lot of misinformation, especially when it comes to sensitive topics like masturbation. This can lead to anxiety and confusion, but many hesitate to bring it up with their healthcare team. This was the case for Chris.

Chris came to see me because he was masturbating regularly and felt shame about it. He was anxious and hesitant, struggling even to mention masturbation during our sessions. He experienced periods where he refrained from masturbating entirely, followed by times when he would masturbate daily. Chris was caught in a cycle of uncertainty, believing that as someone in a regular sexual relationship, he shouldn't need to masturbate.

This kind of anxiety is not uncommon, yet many feel that they should already know the answers and are hesitant to ask an expert. Discussing these concerns with a healthcare professional is crucial for dispelling myths and reducing the unnecessary stress.

In this chapter, we will explore how to address anxiety around masturbation, understand its normalcy, and encourage talking openly with healthcare professionals when you have concerns. The goal is to open up about these issues so we can begin to dismantle the shame and misinformation surrounding masturbation and promote a healthier, more informed approach to sexual health.

UNDERSTANDING THE INFLUENCE

Where did your beliefs about masturbation come from? Whose voice is it that tells you masturbation is wrong? Often, these perceptions are shaped by various sources, including family, religion, and cultural influences, which can sometimes perpetuate misconceptions. Yet, these aren't the only influences.

Often, boys begin masturbating in secret, and masturbation isn't discussed as part of healthy sexuality, so, shame and guilt over masturbating develop.

Media plays a significant role in shaping societal views on masturbation. A simple Google search on the topic yields a range of results, from articles warning about supposed side effects to medical perspectives on its benefits. This abundance of conflicting information can understandably lead to confusion and concern among people seeking clarity. Navigating these conflicting viewpoints can leave you unsure about what to believe.

Beyond media, peer messaging also influences beliefs about masturbation. Conversations among friends or within social circles can either normalize or stigmatize the practice, depending on cultural and social norms.

THE TRUTH ABOUT MASTURBATION

First, I want to highlight that masturbation is a natural, human experience. Whether you engage in masturbation for sexual pleasure, relaxation, or a combination of the two, you are perfectly normal and human.

Much of the rhetoric about masturbation would lead you to believe that it's harmful to your health and relationships, but that's simply not true. I just performed a Google search while writing this chapter and found five resources discussing masturbation as a healthy form of sexual expression and three calling it harmful to your mental and/or physical health.[16] A deeper dive, though, reveals that the articles claiming masturbation is healthy and normal are the ones from reputable peer-reviewed sources.[17] The truth is sexual pleasure is a wonderful part of being human, and you should feel free to enjoy the experience. Here are some things that masturbation provides.[18]

- **Sexual Pleasure:** Masturbation is a means of achieving sexual pleasure and satisfaction.
- **Stress Relief:** It can serve as a way to alleviate stress and tension.
- **Release of Sexual Urges:** In the absence of a partner, masturbation provides a healthy outlet for sexual urges.
- **Sleep Aid:** Some individuals use it as a method to help them relax and fall asleep.
- **Self-Exploration:** Masturbation allows individuals to explore their own bodies, develop self-intimacy, and build self-trust.
- **Exploration of Fantasies:** It provides a safe space to explore sexual fantasies and preferences.

When we understand this as the reality, we can begin to put aside the shame and confusion and enjoy the positive effects of masturbation. Whether experimenting with different techniques or enjoying moments of self-pleasure, the process should be free from worry. Fostering a positive and accepting attitude towards self-pleasure can promote a healthier perspective on sexual health and well-being. So, embrace your own

---

[16] Guinta, C. (2023, October 12). The great masturbation hoax: Is not masturbating unhealthy for you? *Covenant Eyes.* https://www.covenanteyes.com/blog/the-great-masturbation-hoax-is-not-masturbating-unhealthy-for-you/.

[17] Planned Parenthood. (n.d.). *Masturbation.* https://www.plannedparenthood.org/learn/sex-pleasure-and-sexual-dysfunction/masturbation *(Accessed February 2, 2025).*

[18] Regnerus, M., Price, J., & Gordon, D. (2017). Masturbation and partnered sex: Substitutes or complements? *Archives of Sexual Behavior, 46*(7), 2111–2121. https://pubmed.ncbi.nlm.nih.gov/28341933/.

preferences and discover what brings you satisfaction as a natural part of sexual self-discovery.

MINDFUL MASTURBATION: A STEP-BY-STEP GUIDE TO SELF-EXPLORATION AND RELAXATION

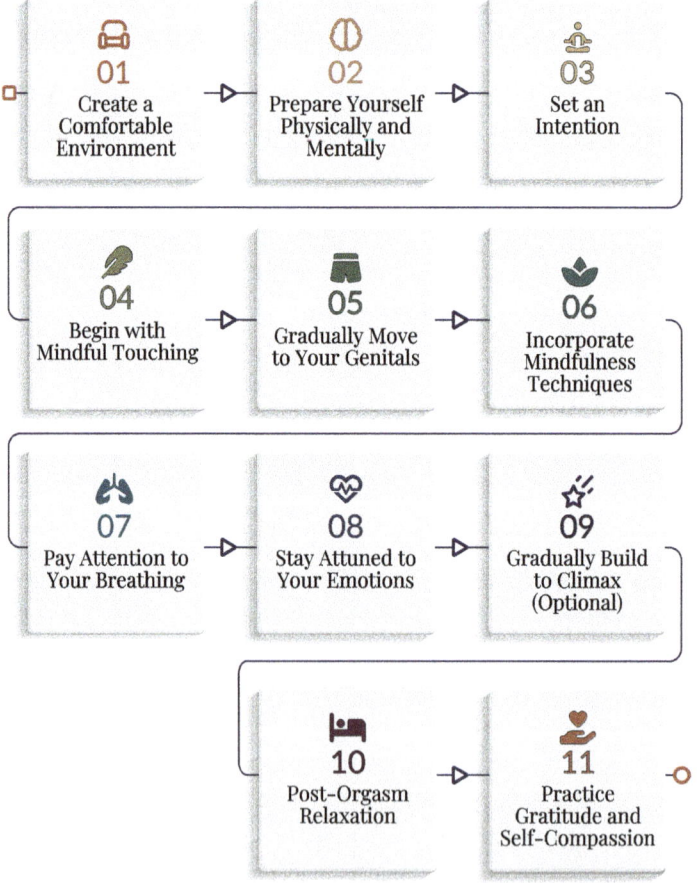

Often, when men in my office discuss masturbation, it's typically because they're worried about the frequency of masturbation, or the urge to self-pleasure. Typically, though, what we actually uncover is trouble remaining present and mindful during sexual experiences (solo or partnered).

Mindful masturbation can be a powerful practice for enhancing self-awareness, relaxation, and self-compassion. Here's a step-by-step process to help you create a meaningful and mindful experience:

Step 1: Create a Comfortable Environment

To begin your mindful masturbation practice, it's essential to create a comfortable and conducive environment:

- **Find a Quiet Space:** Choose a location where you feel safe and free from interruptions.
- **Set the Mood:** Dim the lights, play calming music, or use scented candles to set a relaxing atmosphere.
- **Ensure Privacy:** Make sure you won't be disturbed to fully immerse yourself in the experience.
- **Slow Down:** Allow yourself ample time without feeling rushed, creating a space where you can truly focus on the present moment.

Step 2: Prepare Yourself Physically and Mentally

Preparing yourself both physically and mentally sets the foundation for a mindful experience:

- **Relax Your Body:** Take a warm shower or bath to relax your muscles and clear your mind of any tension.
- **Practice Deep Breathing:** Spend a few moments practicing deep, slow breaths to center yourself and calm any lingering anxiety.
- **Check-In:** Take a moment to check in with yourself. Are you ready to be fully present in the moment? Leave behind any distractions or stressors that may be weighing on your mind.

Step 3: Set an Intention

Setting an intention helps you focus your mind and energies during the practice:

- **Focus on the Experience:** Decide what you wish to achieve from this session—relaxation, self-exploration, or simply enjoying the sensations without any goals.
- **Embrace Self-Compassion:** Remember that this is a time for self-love and acceptance, free from judgments or expectations.
- **Bring Yourself Back:** If your mind begins to wander, gently guide your thoughts back to the present moment and your intention for this practice.

Step 4: Begin with Mindful Touching

Start by exploring your body with mindful touch:

- **Explore Your Body:** Begin by gently touching various parts of your body, focusing on the sensations without rushing.
- **Stay Present:** Notice the texture of your skin, the temperature of your touch, and how your body responds to your gentle caresses.
- **Explore:** Take this opportunity to explore parts of your body that you may not normally touch, allowing yourself to discover new sensations and pleasures.

Step 5: Gradually Move to Your Genitals

When you feel ready, slowly transition your touch to your genitals:

- **Slow and Gentle:** Keep your movements slow and gentle, maintaining your focus on the pleasurable sensations.

- **Vary Your Touch:** Experiment with different types of touch—soft, firm, fast, slow—and observe how each touch feels.

Step 6: Incorporate Mindfulness Techniques

Integrate mindfulness techniques to deepen your experience:

- **Stay Present:** Continuously bring your attention back to the present moment. Focus on your breath and the sensations you're experiencing.
- **Use Visualization:** Visualize energy flowing through your body or imagine a warm light spreading with each touch, enhancing your awareness and pleasure.

Step 7: Pay Attention to Your Breathing

Sync your breath with your touch to enhance relaxation and arousal:

- **Synchronize Your Breath:** Coordinate your breathing with your movements. Deep, rhythmic breathing can amplify sensations and deepen your relaxation.
- **Enhance Pleasure:** As arousal builds, use your breath to intensify the pleasure. Inhale deeply to heighten sensations and exhale slowly to release tension.

Step 8: Stay Attuned to Your Emotions

Acknowledge and embrace your emotions throughout the experience:

- **Notice Feelings:** Observe any emotions that arise—pleasure, discomfort, or anything else—without judgment.
- **Embrace Positivity:** Allow yourself to fully experience positive emotions such as joy and relaxation as you connect with your body.

Step 9: Gradually Build to Climax (Optional)

If you choose to reach orgasm, do so mindfully:

- **Mindful Arousal:** Focus on the build-up of sensations and waves of pleasure, staying present with each moment.
- **Controlled Build-Up:** Bring yourself close to climax and then pause to prolong and deepen the experience, heightening your awareness of each sensation.

Step 10: Post-Orgasm Relaxation

After climax, take time to relax and reflect on your experience:

- **Savor the Moment:** Allow yourself to bask in the afterglow, noticing how your body feels and continuing to breathe deeply.
- **Reflect:** Spend a few moments reflecting on the experience. What did you notice about your body and mind? How do you feel emotionally?

Step 11: Practice Gratitude and Self-Compassion

Conclude your practice with gratitude and kindness towards yourself:

- **Appreciate the Experience:** Show gratitude for the time you dedicated to self-exploration and self-care.
- **Be Kind to Yourself:** Treat yourself with compassion, recognizing the importance of self-love and nurturing your sexual well-being.

This comprehensive step-by-step guide to mindful masturbation helps you embark on a journey to cultivate a profound connection with your body. It allows you to explore and understand your physical responses. It promotes heightened self-awareness of your desires, boundaries, and preferences.

Engaging in mindful masturbation encourages you to be present in the moment, fostering a deeper appreciation for your body's sensations and responses. By focusing on each touch, breath, and sensation, you develop a mindful approach that transcends mere physical pleasure, enriching your overall well-being.

It's a practice that encourages the integration of mindfulness and self-compassion into your sexual expression. It prompts you to approach your body with kindness, free from judgment or expectations. Embracing self-compassion during intimate moments enhances your emotional resilience and nurtures a positive relationship with your sexuality.

Ultimately, mindful masturbation is not just about physical release; it's about nurturing a holistic sense of self. It empowers you to honor your body's needs, explore your sexuality with curiosity and respect, and cultivate a fulfilling path to sexual wellness and self-discovery. If you want more information about mindful masturbation, I urge you to visit my website at www.drmichaelstokes.com where I have an ever-expanding list of tips and techniques as well as guided meditations.

THE ROLE OF THERAPY

Many clients who come to me worried about the role masturbation plays in their lives struggle because of all the mixed messaging they get about it. My goal in these situations is to help clients tune into the Autonomous Sexuality Model from the beginning of this book and use it to create a new paradigm for thinking about self-pleasure.[19]

---

[19] Litam, S. A., & Speciale, M. (2021). Deconstructing sexual shame: Implications for clinical counselors and counselor educators. *Journal of Counseling Sexology & Sexual Wellness: Research, Practice, and Education, 3*(1), 14–24. https://doi.org/10.34296/03011045.

A skilled therapist can provide guidance and support as you navigate through these complexities. They help you explore and dismantle old patterns of shame and restriction, allowing you to develop a healthier relationship with masturbation and your sexuality overall. Seeking support from a sex-positive therapist can facilitate this process, empowering you to embrace a positive and affirming relationship with your sexual identity and well-being and learning to trust your instincts and beliefs, even when they conflict with external opinions from sources like Google, religious teachings, or partners. Here's why seeking therapy with an AASECT-certified therapist can be instrumental in this process.[20]

Trusting Your Judgment

The journey towards trusting yourself begins with acknowledging that you know yourself best. This involves understanding and honoring your own values, desires, and boundaries despite societal or cultural norms that may suggest otherwise. It means having confidence in your ability to make decisions that align with your personal well-being and happiness.

The Challenge of Self-Trust

However, developing self-trust is often not something that can be achieved alone. Despite efforts to build confidence and self-assurance independently, ingrained emotional and behavioral patterns can be deeply rooted and difficult to unravel without external support.

---

[20] Goffnett, J., Liechty, J. M., & Kidder, E. (2020). Interventions to reduce shame: A systematic review. *Journal of Behavioral and Cognitive Therapy, 30*(2), 141–160. https://doi.org/10.1016/j.jbct.2020.03.001.

What Therapy Provides

Therapy provides a supportive and non-judgmental environment where you can explore and challenge long-standing beliefs and behaviors that no longer serve you. A skilled therapist can help you examine areas of your life where you've experienced mistrust, whether in relationships, emotions, or personal identity.

For many men, societal messages from a young age, such as "don't cry," can undermine trust in their own emotional responses—the very core of their humanity. Therapy offers a structured approach to relearning trust in oneself, fostering a deeper understanding and acceptance of your authentic self.

Undoing Emotional Barriers

Therapy facilitates the process of undoing emotional barriers and cultivating self-trust by:

- **Exploring Emotional Responses:** Encouraging you to reconnect with and trust your innate emotional responses, which are fundamental to personal authenticity.
- **Addressing Long-Standing Patterns:** Helping you identify and modify patterns of behavior and thought that inhibit self-trust and personal growth.
- **Providing Guidance:** Offering guidance and tools to navigate conflicting external influences and make decisions that honor your true self.

Building self-trust is a deeply personal journey. Therapy offers invaluable support and guidance along the way. It provides a safe space to explore, heal, and ultimately empower yourself to make decisions about your sexual health and well-being from a place of confidence and self-assurance.

CHRIS AND HIS PROGRESS IN THERAPY

I opened this chapter with the story of Chris. Let's revisit his journey and see the concerns he addressed in therapy.

During our sessions, Chris and I navigated through the shame surrounding masturbation. By using mindful masturbation as a guide, Chris began his journey, which involved addressing common misconceptions and providing clarity on what constitutes healthy sexual practices. We discussed several taboo topics that Chris raised, seeking understanding and guidance. Here are some of the questions he had:

Frequency of Masturbation

One of Chris's concerns was understanding what constitutes a healthy frequency for masturbation. This is a common question among individuals who may feel uncertain about their habits and whether they align with healthy norms. We discussed that the frequency of masturbation varies widely among individuals and is influenced by personal preferences, libido, and relationship status. There is no one-size-fits-all answer. It's about finding a balance that feels comfortable and respectful of your own needs and lifestyle.

Use of Semen

Chris also inquired about whether there are health considerations regarding the release of semen during masturbation. Specifically, he questioned whether it should be reserved for sexual encounters with a partner. We discussed that masturbation is a natural and healthy way to release sexual tension and does not pose any health risks regarding semen release. Semen production is a continuous process in the body, and its release through masturbation or sexual intercourse is a normal part of sexual health.

Health Implications of Masturbation

Another concern Chris raised was whether masturbation could cause any health issues. This is a common misconception rooted in misinformation or cultural taboos. We explored that, in fact, masturbation is a safe and normal activity that can have positive effects on sexual health, including stress relief and improved mood. There is no evidence to suggest that moderate masturbation leads to negative health outcomes; however, excessive or compulsive behaviors may warrant further evaluation.

Communication and Boundaries

Navigating discussions about masturbation within a relationship can be sensitive and complex, as each individual's comfort levels and perspectives vary. Chris's experience highlights two distinct approaches to managing this aspect of sexual expression:

Keeping Masturbation Private

For Chris, maintaining masturbation as a solo activity without discussing specific details with his partner was essential. When asked how he would respond if his wife inquired about his masturbation habits, Chris emphasized honesty tempered with privacy:

- **Honesty and Boundaries:** Chris expressed that he would truthfully acknowledge his solo practice of masturbation if asked, but he also recognized the importance of maintaining boundaries. He felt it unnecessary to provide extensive details or announce each occurrence, viewing masturbation as a personal aspect of his sexuality.
- **Respecting Individual Space:** Masturbation for Chris was not a secretive activity but rather a private one, emphasizing the

distinction between personal sexual exploration and shared intimacy within the relationship.

Conversely, another approach involves open communication with your partner about any discomfort or uncertainties surrounding masturbation:

- **Addressing Unsettling Feelings:** If you experience unsettling feelings about masturbation, discussing these emotions with your partner can promote understanding and mutual respect. Communicate why masturbation is significant to your sexual identity and reassure your partner that it complements—not competes with—your shared sexual experiences.
- **Differentiating Between Intimacies:** It's crucial to convey that masturbation is distinct from partnered sexual encounters. Assure your partner that your intimacy together is cherished and unique, affirming their pleasure and enjoyment during shared sexual experiences.

In some relationships, concerns may arise if one partner feels their masturbation habits are scrutinized or controlled:

- **Clarifying Differences:** Open dialogue is essential in clarifying why masturbation differs from partnered sex. Emphasize that masturbation is a natural part of sexual health and individual pleasure, distinct from the emotional and physical connection shared with a partner.
- **Reassuring Your Partner:** Assure your partner that their satisfaction and pleasure are priorities during shared sexual experiences, reinforcing the understanding that masturbation serves personal needs and does not diminish intimacy together.

The Progress of Therapy

By addressing these questions and concerns, Chris and I were able to dismantle the shame and misinformation surrounding masturbation. Providing education on what constitutes healthy masturbation practices empowered Chris to make informed decisions about his sexual health and well-being. These discussions illustrate the importance of open dialogue and accurate information in promoting a positive attitude towards sexual self-care and overall wellness.

Ultimately, the approach to discussing masturbation within a relationship should align with mutual respect, trust, and understanding. Whether maintaining privacy as a personal choice or engaging in open communication to address concerns, fostering a supportive environment where both partners feel valued and secure in their sexual identities is paramount. By navigating these conversations with sensitivity and honesty, couples can strengthen their bond and cultivate a healthy approach to sexual intimacy and individual fulfillment.

FINDING A SEX-POSITIVE THERAPIST

When seeking a therapist who understands and supports your sexual health and well-being, it's essential to look for specific qualities and specializations. Here are vital aspects to consider when searching for a sex-positive therapist:

Trauma-Informed Approach

A trauma-informed therapist is crucial, especially when addressing sensitive topics related to sexuality. They possess the knowledge and skills to handle trauma-related issues sensitively and effectively, ensuring your emotional safety throughout the therapeutic process.

Client-Focused Practice

A therapist who prioritizes a client-focused approach tailors their therapy to meet your individual needs and goals. They create a supportive environment where you feel heard, understood, and empowered to explore and address your concerns about sexuality.

Sex-Positive Philosophy

Seek out therapists who are certified by the American Association of Sexuality Educators, Counselors and Therapists (AASECT). This organization provides training, community, and visibility to promote the understanding of human sexuality and healthy sexual behavior.

While many therapists may identify as sex-positive, the specialized training of an AASECT therapist means you're getting expert advice from someone who views sexual diversity as natural and healthy, promoting open discussions and positive attitudes about sexual expression.

Specialization in Men's Issues

Given your specific needs, consider therapists who specialize in working with men. These therapists have expertise in addressing the unique challenges and concerns that men may face regarding sexuality, masculinity, relationships, and personal development.

As you consider masturbation in a healthy light, it's natural for your behaviors and attitudes to evolve accordingly. Here's how a change in perspective can influence your behavior:

Overcoming Shame and Confusion

Consider how labeling behaviors or activities, like eating cookies, can impact your actions. If you view cookies as "bad" and strictly limit yourself from enjoying them, you might find yourself fixating on them.

This can lead to moments of overindulgence, such as consuming an entire order of Girl Scout cookies in one sitting when they finally arrive in April. This cycle often stems from feelings of shame and the perceived need for strict restriction.

So, if you tell yourself you're not allowed to masturbate at all or that masturbation is bad or evil, you're more likely to struggle, cave in, and feel the shame cycle return.

Embracing Moderation

Adopting a mindset that allows for moderation can transform your approach. Instead of labeling masturbation—or cookies—as inherently negative or off-limits, consider integrating it into your life in a balanced way. Just as enjoying a couple of cookies each day can prevent the urge to binge, viewing masturbation as a natural part of your sexual health can alleviate feelings of shame and reduce compulsive behaviors.

CHAPTER TAKEAWAYS

- Masturbation is a normal and healthy aspect of sexuality.
- Practicing mindful masturbation fosters a better relationship with the body and reduces anxiety.
- Recognizing unhealthy patterns allows for a more fulfilling and intentional solo experience.

CHAPTER 6

AM I GAY? STRAIGHT? BI? DOES IT MATTER?

Sexuality is more complex than some realize. People can identify themselves romantically and sexually in many ways. This is why it is crucial to develop an understanding of sexual orientation and appreciate the variety of experiences. It's not just about labels but about how individuals feel attracted to others and how these feelings can evolve over time.

Recent research has shown that sexual orientation isn't fixed—it can change as people grow and experience different relationships and situations. This challenges the idea that sexual identity is always set in stone and shows that it can be influenced by personal experiences and societal norms.

Questioning fixed ideas about sexual orientation helps us understand that it's OK for feelings and attractions to shift. This concept, known as sexual fluidity, recognizes that people may feel differently at different points in their lives. It encourages us to create inclusive spaces where everyone's identity is respected and accepted.

So take a deep breath. Relax. I know this is not an easy topic for everyone, especially if you were raised with rigid ideas of sexuality. Yet, there are valuable things to learn. It's OK to challenge these rigid ideas and deepen our understanding of sexuality.

In this chapter, we will explore these ideas further. We'll discuss how diverse sexual orientations are understood and experienced. We'll also see why it's important to support individuals in exploring and defining their identities without judgment. By learning from research and experts, we aim to promote understanding and create a more inclusive society where everyone can freely express who they are. So join me as we navigate the multidimensional complexities of male sexuality.

BEN'S STORY

A few years ago, Ben came to talk to me. He sat nervously with an anxious expression. I soon found out why when he said he wanted to talk about his porn use.

"Is it how often you watch?" I asked.

"No."

"Is it how long you watch?"

"No."

"Is it the type of porn you watch?"

"Yes," he said, taking a deep breath. "This is really hard to talk about. I can't believe I'm saying it out loud, but I watched gay porn last week. I got aroused and finished, and I've been freaking out since."

I asked him to explain more about his anxiety. He said, "I can't stop thinking that I'm gay. I've been acting weird around my girlfriend, and she keeps noticing that I'm not really present. I haven't watched any porn since because I'm scared of what's going to happen."

When I asked him about his fear, Ben explained, "I'm afraid that I won't be aroused by straight porn anymore, and I'll have to watch gay porn because that's what aroused me last time."

He then talked about times in his past that he thought might mean he was gay, like playing with his sister's dolls, being very attached to his mom, and an incident in fourth grade when a kid flashed him in the bathroom. At this point, Ben was spiraling.

To help him calm down, I asked about the reasons he didn't think he was gay. He started to relax and said, "I've been in a relationship with my girlfriend for a year and a half. We have a great relationship and a great sex life. I haven't been sexually attracted to guys before. I was friends with a gay guy in college, and nothing happened between us."

I asked him to think about what happened the day he watched the gay porn. He said, "I had some time because my girlfriend was at the store. I put on the usual stuff I enjoy, and then an ad came up with two guys. I clicked on it, and it brought me to a gay porn video. I didn't turn it off. I continued to masturbate and finished within forty-five seconds of watching that video."

After he shared this, I checked in with him. "That was a lot of information. How does it feel to get all of that out?"

He paused and said, "It's actually a relief."

I asked him where he felt this relief in his body, and he said his shoulders were not as tense. When I asked why he felt more relaxed, he said, "I was able to tell you that, and you didn't make a weird face. I don't think you're judging me."

I told him we were going to be able to figure this out. "Do you feel hopeful?"

"Yes," he said.

I reflected on what he had told me. "You had some time, turned on porn, probably horny before you started. You began to watch and masturbate, and then, already aroused, a different type of sex image played. It may not have been what you usually watch, but it's still designed to cause arousal. Plus, it was something new, so you were curious. You continued to masturbate, and your body responded normally. The real issue is the high level of anxiety and worry you're feeling, not the gay porn you watched for forty-five seconds."

Ben thought about this and said, "I'm not supposed to watch that. Only gay people watch gay porn. If I watch it and enjoy it, it must mean I'm gay."

Sexuality isn't that simple.

UNDERSTANDING SEXUAL ORIENTATION

In 1948, biologist Alfred Kinsey published a groundbreaking report that forever changed the way society understood human sexuality.[21] Known as the Kinsey Reporor the Kinsey Scale, his work challenged common beliefs about sexual orientation and behavior. Kinsey's research introduced the idea that sexual orientation exists on a continuum rather than a strict binary of heterosexual and homosexual.

The report, titled "Sexual Behavior in the Human Male," was based on extensive interviews with thousands of men about their sexual experiences and desires. Kinsey and his team found that many men reported same-sex attractions or experiences at some point in their lives, challenging the notion that homosexuality was rare or abnormal. This finding was revolutionary in a time when homosexuality was largely stigmatized and considered taboo.

The Kinsey Scale placed individuals on a spectrum of sexual orientation ranging from exclusively heterosexual to exclusively homosexual, with varying degrees of bisexuality in between. This scale provided a framework for understanding that sexual orientation is not rigid but fluid and can change over time.

The Kinsey Scale sparked widespread debate and controversy, but it also paved the way for more open discussions about sexuality and a deeper understanding of human diversity. By challenging societal norms and promoting scientific inquiry into sexual behavior, Alfred Kinsey's work laid the foundation for later research on sexuality. It paved the way for advancements in LGBTQIA+ rights and acceptance.

Alfred Kinsey's 1948 report on sexuality was a groundbreaking milestone in the study of human behavior. It challenged stereotypes and opened up new avenues for understanding and respecting sexual

---

[21] Kinsey, A. C., Pomeroy, W. B., & Martin, C. E. (1998). *Sexual behavior in the human male*. Indiana University Press. (Original work published 1948).

diversity. His contributions continue to influence research, education, and advocacy for sexual rights today.

Fifty years later, sexologists expanded on Kinsey's ideas. The consensus these days is that human sexuality is much more expansive. The internet, with its vast array of sexual content, has shown just how diverse sexual interests and behaviors can be. Over time, Americans have started to recognize and accept more types of sexual diversity. We've even started creating new language to support the diversity. The term heteroflexible is used by some who have bisexual tendencies, but prefer opposite sex partners.[22] Today, many people start their sex lives before getting married. Most people know someone who is gay. You can buy sex toys at stores like Walmart, and masturbation is now seen as healthy. Each of these changes shows how society is becoming more aware and accepting of different aspects of human sexuality.

INSIGHTS FROM RESEARCH AND EXPERTS

Sexual fluidity is the idea that someone's sexual orientation can change over time or in different situations. This challenges the belief that sexual orientation is permanently fixed and shows how diverse human sexuality can be. Let's hear from some additional experts and research in the area of sexual fluidity:

A study titled "The Current State of Sexual Fluidity Research" suggests that sexual orientation isn't always the same throughout life.[23] It can shift based on personal experiences, relationships, and

---

[22] Carrillo, H., & Hoffman, A. (2018). Straight with a pinch of bi: The construction of heterosexuality as an elastic category among adult US men. *Sexualities, 21*(1–2), 90–108. https://doi.org/10.1177/1363460716678561.

[23] Katz-Wise, S. L., & Todd, K. P. (2022). The current state of sexual fluidity research. *Current Opinion in Psychology, 48*, 101497. https://doi.org/10.1016/j.copsyc.2022.101497.

surroundings. This research shows that sexual orientation can be flexible and vary from person to person.

Sabra L. Katz-Wise, PhD, who co-directs the Harvard Sexual Orientation and Gender Identity and Expression (SOGIE) Health Equity Research Collaborative discusses sexual fluidity in depth. She explains how sexual orientation can change and how this challenges the idea of fixed identities. In fact, 52% of men surveyed in her 2013 study reported shifts in attraction, meaning sometimes they felt attracted to women and sometimes felt attraction toward men.[24] Understanding sexual fluidity helps us respect and support people with different sexual orientations.

THE CONVERSATION CONTINUES

During our sessions, I asked Ben to think about something. "What if you are a straight guy who just stumbled on new porn content that you found arousing? This isn't a question . . . It's a statement. What do you think about that?"

Then, I gave him an example. "Imagine your gay friend from college watches gay porn, clicks on a pop-up for straight porn, and enjoys it for forty-five seconds. Then, he calls me, panicking, thinking he's straight. How could he be gay and finish while watching straight porn?"

Ben laughed and said, "That sounds stupid."

I asked, "Why does that sound stupid, but your situation feels so different? What's the difference?"

Ben thought for a moment and replied, "Because there aren't all these judgments about being straight, but the label of gay is something I've been taught to fear."

---

[24] Katz-Wise, S. L. (2014). Sexual fluidity in young adult women and men: Associations with sexual orientation and sexual identity development. *Psychology & Sexuality, 6*(2), 189–208. https://doi.org/10.1080/19419899.2013.876445.

"So we're really here because society messed you up," I said, smiling.

He laughed again, and then we started the real work of breaking down his fear and panic about being gay.

I asked Ben to tell me about other porn content he had watched that he found arousing but didn't go back to or enjoy in real life. This process helped him understand what happened without the anxiety, worry, and overthinking getting in the way.

In the end, Ben realized that he was just a straight guy who had stumbled on a new type of content he hadn't seen before. Through our discussions, he was able to understand his reactions better and let go of the unnecessary fear and anxiety.

UNDERSTANDING INTERNALIZED HOMOPHOBIA AND FLUID SEXUALITY

During our sessions, Ben faced the fear of being gay, known as homophobia. This fear comes from societal norms and expectations. While many people may not fully understand this, Ben started to see the idea of fluid male sexuality and began to accept it.

It's not unusual for men to express being upset about enjoying gay porn, having a single experience with another man, or finding certain characteristics in men attractive. They start to worry, thinking they might be gay. It's important to know that humans have created labels to understand and define sexuality, but these labels are socially constructed and don't always reflect the true complexity of human sexuality. To be clear, you can enjoy watching gay porn, and even find some men attractive, and not be gay.

Internalized homophobia is common. Almost all my conversations with men, and especially with gay men, reveal some level of homophobia. We need to recognize it, name it, and understand where it came from. We must acknowledge that we grew up in a society that values being straight. Any deviation, like enjoying gay porn, can make a man feel "less than."

We were all raised in a heteronormative society, which means we were taught to value being straight and to assume everyone is straight unless they say otherwise. For example, jokes about a male preschooler having a girlfriend might seem harmless, but if someone said he had a boyfriend, would it feel the same? This shows how deeply ingrained these assumptions are.

No matter what our sexual orientation is, many of us make straight-assuming comments about and to our children. This doesn't mean you hate gay people; it means you have been socialized in a society that places straight people at a higher value than gay people. Part of our work is to acknowledge this bias, question our assumptions, decide if they fit our current values, and then choose to act differently.

Understanding and addressing internalized homophobia is crucial. It allows individuals to understand their feelings and reactions without societal judgment. Ben's journey shows how recognizing and challenging these internalized beliefs can lead to greater self-acceptance and mental well-being.

EXPLORING SEXUAL ORIENTATION AND QUESTIONING

Many men question their sexual orientation after having same-sex experiences during their teenage years, experimenting in college, choosing certain types of porn, or enjoying anal stimulation, either with or without a partner. These experiences can lead to confusion about their true sexual orientation.

This confusion can lead to distress. That's why it's important to provide education and promote understanding. Sexual orientation is complex and varied. Referring again to the Kinsey Scale, we see that sexual orientation exists on a spectrum rather than fitting into strict categories. Here is how the scale is defined:

RATING	DESCRIPTION
0	Exclusively heterosexual
1	Predominantly heterosexual, only incidentally homosexual
2	Predominantly heterosexual, but more than incidentally homosexual
3	Equally heterosexual and homosexual
4	Predominantly homosexual, but more than incidentally heterosexual
5	Predominantly homosexual, only incidentally heterosexual
6	Exclusively homosexual
X	No socio-sexual contacts and reactions

These categories are socially constructed, meaning that they were created by society to help us understand and describe sexual orientation, but they don't capture the full diversity of human experiences.

Labels and Identities

In addition to the Kinsey Scale, there are several common terms people use to describe their sexual orientation:

- **Straight:** Attracted exclusively to the opposite gender.
- **Bisexual (Bi):** Attracted to both men and women.
- **Pansexual (Pan):** Attracted to people regardless of their gender.
- **Gay:** Attracted exclusively to the same gender.
- **Asexual:** Experiences little or no sexual attraction to others.

- **Queer:** A broad term that can include a variety of sexual orientations and gender identities that are not exclusively heterosexual or cisgender.

Anal Play and Sexual Orientation

Interestingly, data shows that a significant percentage of men enjoy anal play as recipients, which does not define their sexual orientation. Enjoying certain sexual activities, like anal play, does not automatically categorize someone as gay or straight.

Expanding Understanding

Sexual orientation is more fluid and complex than simple labels can capture. Understanding this can help reduce the confusion and questioning that many men experience. Recognizing the broad spectrum of human sexuality can create a more inclusive and accepting society where individuals feel comfortable exploring and understanding their own sexual identities.

EXPLORING YOUR FEELINGS

When it comes to your sexual orientation, what matters most is how you feel and how you see yourself. This journey is deeply personal and can be influenced by your experiences and reflections.

Embracing Flexibility

Some people identify as "heteroflexible," meaning they mostly consider themselves straight but are open to having sexual experiences with people of the same gender. Others might describe themselves as "straight-ish," indicating that they typically prefer the opposite sex but may feel differently under certain circumstances.

Questioning Your Sexuality

If you're uncertain about your sexuality, it's important to pay attention to your thoughts and feelings without judging yourself. This introspection can be challenging to navigate alone, which is why seeking help from a professional can be beneficial.

A trained professional can create a supportive environment where you can explore your thoughts and feelings about your sexual orientation. Therapists can help you understand your emotions without bias, allowing you to gain clarity and confidence in defining your identity.

You have the right to define your sexual orientation however you want. I have friends who identify as bisexual and heteroromantic—they have sex with people of multiple genders but only want romantic relationships with opposite gender folks.

Defining your sexual orientation is a personal journey that requires self-reflection and acceptance. Embracing the idea that sexuality can be fluid and seeking guidance when needed can help navigate this process with greater understanding and ease. Remember, the most important thing is how you feel and how you choose to understand your own sexual identity.

CHAPTER TAKEAWAYS

Throughout this chapter, we've explored the diverse ways people experience and understand their sexual orientation. The research leads us to the following understandings:

- **Sexual Orientation Varies:** People experience sexual orientation differently, ranging from being attracted to one gender to experiencing changes over time.
- **Change Is Normal:** Research shows that sexual orientation can shift throughout life due to personal experiences and relationships.
- **Questioning Fixed Ideas:** Understanding sexual fluidity challenges the idea that sexual orientation is always fixed. It acknowledges that attractions and feelings can evolve.
- **Creating Supportive Spaces:** It's important to create environments where all sexual orientations are respected and accepted. This inclusivity helps everyone feel valued and understood.
- **Seeking Help:** If you're unsure about your sexual orientation, talking to a supportive professional who understands LGBTQIA+ issues can provide guidance and clarity.

CHAPTER 7

HOW DO I FIGURE OUT WHAT I REALLY WANT IN MY SEX LIFE?

Adam walked into my office with a common plea among many of my clients: "I just want more sex." His straightforward request is a refrain I hear often, echoing the frustrations and desires of many men seeking to enhance their sexual experiences. Yet, as we delved deeper, it became clear that Adam's understanding of "more" wasn't just about frequency.

"What does 'more' mean for you?" I asked, encouraging him to think beyond the number of encounters.

"I want to have sex more times every week," Adam replied, his answer initially skimming the surface.

"And what about the kind of sex—the quality of it?" I probed further, aiming to shift his focus from quantity to quality.

He paused, a look of contemplation crossing his face. "I've never thought about that before."

This was the opening I needed to introduce Adam to a more profound exploration of his desires. "What if the issue isn't just about quantity, but quality—the level of connection, intimacy, exploration, and openness?"

From there, we embarked on a visualization exercise to map out his ideal sex life, considering not just frequency but the richness of his sexual engagements:

Adam's ideal vision included having sex three times a week, with each encounter featuring mutual oral sex, fostering a space where he could feel comfortable discussing his desires with his wife without fear of awkwardness or pressure—a common fear rooted in the dread of rejection.

NAVIGATING COMMUNICATION AND NEGOTIATION

Mapping out an ideal sex life is a nuanced journey, particularly when a partner is involved. For many, like Adam, the challenge lies in bringing these desires into conversations with their partners. Concerns about judgment or being misunderstood as merely sex-driven can stifle open communication.

"What's stopping you?" I asked, addressing the elephant in the room—communication barriers.

"I can't talk to my wife about this. She'll judge me, think I'm a sex-crazed guy who wants it all the time," Adam confessed, voicing his fears.

Challenging these notions one by one, we explored how straightforward communication might seem daunting yet is incredibly effective. "What if you said, 'Hey, we don't talk about our sex life much. I really want to have meaningful sex with you that we both enjoy'?" I suggested, providing him with simpler, direct language to break the ice.

"That seems way too easy—I don't have the words to communicate that," Adam hesitated, a common initial resistance born from vulnerability.

Providing the language and skills necessary to express these thoughts is crucial. I equipped Adam with phrases and encouraged a vulnerability that fosters deeper connections and understanding between partners.

EMBRACING A FULLER EXPERIENCE

As we continued our sessions, Adam began to see the importance of not just aiming for more sex, but better sex—sex that is enriching, satisfying, and integrative of both partners' desires and fears. This realization opened a new pathway for him, one where sexual experiences became a source of connection rather than just physical satisfaction.

Beyond Frequency: Expanding the Definition

Do you think of sex as the act of putting a penis into a vagina? If so, you're in good company. Many of the men I work with come into my office with this view of sex. The problem? This limits sex to the act of procreation. It makes sex something that you do a few times a month rather than an experience you enjoy.

But, what if sex could mean so much more? What if sex could be playful, fun, romantic, dangerous, dirty, naughty, energizing? To start exploring your definition of sex, in an effort to map out your ideal sex life, I encourage you to try out some things from these categories.

- **Sensory Pleasure:** Exploring touch in different areas of your body and your partner's body. Touching with hands, with toys, with lotion, and without. Try incorporating temperature play.

Add an ice cube to your mouth or hand, or warm the massage oil you use that day.
- **Fantasy Exploration:** Explore a new fantasy. You can do this on your own, with erotic audio, porn, or erotic literature. Try it on your own first, then, if you enjoy it, consider including our partner. What fantasies have you never explored?
- **Erotic Communication:** When I talk about erotic communication with my clients they sometimes assume I mean sexting or dirty talk. And, while that is certainly one way to communicate, I want to ask you to go a bit further. Completing a yes, no, maybe chart for yourself, having your partner do the same, and then comparing the two can help you deepen your understanding of our sexual self and give you ideas about what to try.

Designing your ideal sex life is about more than fulfilling a quota; it's about creating experiences that resonate on deeper emotional, psychological, and relational levels. For Adam, and for many others, the journey begins with redefining what "more" truly means—transforming it from a measure of frequency to a gauge of fulfillment and connection. This chapter aims to guide you through this transformative process, helping you craft a sex life that not only meets but exceeds your deepest desires.

CHAPTER TAKEAWAYS

- Creating a personal vision for sex helps align experiences with desires and values.
- Communicating sexual wants and boundaries strengthens relationships.
- Sexual fulfillment is an evolving process rather than a fixed destination.

CHAPTER 8

WHY DO I SOMETIMES WANT SEX AND OTHER TIMES I DON'T?

"It's been seven years since we had sex," Roger sat with his hands folded in his lap, staring at the place where his fingers intertwined.

His wife, Alice, sat with her hands pressed under her thighs, refusing to meet my gaze. "It just . . . it feels like we're roommates more than anything else. I don't know how we got here, but it seems like maybe we just don't want the same things anymore."

"I just feel like you don't even want me to touch you anymore," Roger said.

Alice sighed, finally meeting my eyes before turning to Roger. "That's not true. I do want intimacy I just thought you weren't interested anymore. You never said anything, so I stopped asking.

Alice and Roger, like so many couples I meet, made quiet assumptions about one another. I asked them to open up a bit more. "Can you tell me what led you to that conclusion?"

"Every night we just went to bed without touching, without talking about it. Days turned into months and then years. I just figured if Roger wanted me, he would've said something," Alice looked back at the ground.

Roger jumped in quickly "I thought the same about you. I felt like maybe you didn't find me attractive anymore, or that you were just putting up with me. I didn't want to pressure you or make you feel uncomfortable."

It's quite common for couples to fall into this pattern of non-communication, especially about such sensitive topics (and penises, vaginas, and all the cooperating parts are definitely sensitive). Both Roger and Alice were waiting for the other to make a move, which led to a stalemate. What they describe is what we call *unseen desires*—both Roger and Alice have desire for one another, but they let lack of communication take over.

Alice slowly starts to meet Roger's gaze. "I didn't realize you felt that way. I . . . I've missed you. I just didn't know how to bring it up without making things awkward or facing rejection."

"I've missed you too. I guess we both got caught up in our fears."

"I'm just not sure where to start."

Let's start with understanding the types of desire.

THE SPECTRUM OF DESIRE

Understanding desire in relationships means recognizing its different forms: responsive and spontaneous desire.

Responsive Desire is akin to a slow burn that needs an external spark to ignite. It's not about the absence of desire but rather the need for specific conditions to feel it. This could mean long hugs, thoughtful conversations, or shared activities that build emotional connection and set the stage for physical intimacy.

Spontaneous Desire, on the other hand, is immediate and often unexpected—it's the "see it, want it" kind of desire. It can be triggered by a simple gesture, an alluring glance, or even casual nudity. This type of desire doesn't require the build-up that responsive desire does; it's ready to go at a moment's notice.

BRIDGING THE DESIRE GAP

In my practice, I often see couples struggling to synchronize their types of desire, which can lead to feelings of rejection or dissatisfaction. Understanding which type of desire you and your partner lean towards can dramatically improve how you connect sexually. The goal is to meet in the middle, ensuring both partners feel fulfilled.

For example, a couple I worked with—both busy professionals with a child—found themselves misaligned in their desires due to their hectic schedules. This couple, a lawyer and a doctor, rarely had time to engage in the type of extensive foreplay that one partner, who primarily experienced responsive desire, needed to feel ready for intimacy. Their story underscores the importance of making time for one another, slowing down to notice and appreciate each other's needs and desires.

ROGER AND HIS WIFE'S JOURNEY

Returning to Roger and his wife, their journey to rediscovering sexual intimacy involved several steps, starting with identifying and understanding their own patterns of desire. They began with simple activities like sharing a shower, engaging in longer hugs, and spending quiet evenings together without the pressure of sexual performance. These activities served as cues for the partner with responsive desire, while also satisfying the need for spontaneity for the partner with spontaneous desire.

As they continued to communicate and experiment with ways to meet each other's needs, they found a new rhythm to their sexual relationship, one that included both planned and spontaneous encounters.

ADAPTING TO LIFE'S CHANGES

Desire can fluctuate throughout life, influenced by external pressures such as work stress, parenting responsibilities, or caring for aging parents. In these moments, spontaneous desire can take a back seat, but that doesn't mean intimacy has to fade. Instead, couples can find new ways to connect, whether that means seizing quiet moments during a child's nap (or an episode of Bluey) or prioritizing small acts of affection when life feels chaotic.

Beyond external stressors, physical changes also play a significant role in how people experience intimacy. For women, postpartum recovery can bring shifts in body image, hormonal fluctuations, and physical discomfort that may affect desire and confidence in the bedroom. The body has just gone through a transformation—stretching, healing, and adjusting—and it's common for new mothers to feel differently about physical intimacy. Partners who approach this time with patience, reassurance, and open communication will foster a sense of connection even when sex isn't immediately back to "normal."

On the other end of the spectrum, aging brings its own set of changes. Hormonal shifts, reduced testosterone levels, and changes in circulation can impact libido and sexual function for people of all genders. But rather than seeing these changes as barriers, they can be an opportunity to redefine what intimacy means. Exploring new types of touch, communication, and non-penetrative forms of connection can keep desire alive, even when the body doesn't respond the same way it once did.

By recognizing that intimacy evolves over time, couples can approach their sex life with curiosity instead of frustration. Whether navigating early parenthood or the later stages of life, adapting together fosters resilience, closeness, and a deeper understanding of each other's evolving needs.

TOOLS FOR NURTURING DESIRE

Neither Alice nor Roger could address their desire as a couple without first evaluating their desire for sex as individuals. There are a few ways to reconnect with your sexual self, but these are my favorite and the ones I've found most effective in practice.

Somatic Exercises

Somatic exercises are powerful tools for reconnecting with your body, enhancing awareness, and deepening intimacy, both with yourself and your partner. These exercises focus on the experience of bodily sensations and can help individuals and couples cultivate a greater sense of presence, reduce anxiety (a huge killer of desire), and increase sexual and emotional intimacy.

Solo Somatic Exercises

1. **Mindful Breathing:** This is a foundational practice for becoming present in your body. Sit or lie down in a comfortable position. Close your eyes and focus on your breath. Notice the sensation of air entering and leaving your body. Observe the rise and fall of your chest or abdomen. This practice can help calm the mind and bring your awareness back to your body, making it a great precursor to more intimate moments.
2. **Body Scan Meditation:** Lie down in a quiet space. Starting at the top of your head, slowly bring your attention to each part of your body. Notice any sensations, tensions, or emotions

that arise. Don't judge or try to change these sensations; simply observe them. This exercise increases bodily awareness and can enhance your ability to experience pleasure during sexual activity.
3. **Somatic Dancing:** Put on music that you feel drawn to. Let your body move freely without planning or judgment. Focus on how your body wants to move with the rhythm. This exercise helps release bodily tensions, increases energy flow, and improves body confidence.

Partnered Somatic Exercises

1. **Mirror Exercises:** Sit or stand facing your partner. Begin to mimic each other's movements in a slow, mindful manner. This exercise helps build empathy and emotional attunement, making you more receptive to each other's nonverbal cues in intimate settings.
2. **Synchronized Breathing:** Sit facing each other, close enough to feel each other's breath. Align your breathing so that you inhale and exhale together. You can place your hands on each other's heart or hold hands to enhance the connection. This exercise builds intimacy and can be a profound prelude to deeper sexual connection.
3. **Eye Gazing:** Sit comfortably facing your partner and gaze into each other's eyes without talking. Start with one minute and gradually increase the duration. Eye gazing is a powerful tool for creating emotional intimacy and can often lead to increased sexual desire and connection.

Combined Solo and Partnered Exercises

1. **Progressive Muscle Relaxation (PMR):** Tense each muscle group in your body for five seconds and then relax for thirty

seconds. Progress through each part of your body from your feet to your head. If done with a partner, you can take turns guiding each other through the exercise. PMR reduces physical and mental tension and enhances sensitivity to touch.
2. **Sensate Focus:** This exercise involves touching and being touched by your partner in a non-sexual way to build trust and increase intimacy. Start with non-genital areas, focusing solely on the sensation of touch. Swap roles and discuss the experience afterward, sharing what felt good or what you were sensitive to. Sensate focus is beneficial for couples dealing with sexual dysfunction or those looking to deepen their physical and emotional connection.
3. **Guided Imagery:** This can be used to visualize calming or erotic scenarios. This exercise involves describing a scene in detail to yourself or your partner, focusing on sensory experiences and emotional feelings. It helps in reducing performance anxiety and increasing mental engagement with sexual and intimate activities.

These somatic exercises are designed to bridge the gap between mind and body, helping individuals and couples foster a deeper connection to their physical selves and each other. By regularly practicing these exercises, you can enhance your ability to engage fully in the present moment, both in and out of intimate contexts.

Scheduled Intimacy

Use digital calendars or set phone reminders to schedule intimate moments. This could be as simple as sending a thoughtful text or planning a regular date night. These scheduled times serve as a commitment to maintain and nurture your relationship.

Scheduling intimacy helps ensure that busy schedules do not interfere with emotional and physical connection. It creates anticipation and shows a dedicated effort to prioritize the relationship, enhancing emotional bonds and sexual desire over time.

Daily Touch

Integrate small acts of physical affection into your daily routine. Hold hands while watching TV, give a back rub while your partner reads, or simply touch their arm or shoulder as you walk past. Make a habit of greeting each other with a hug or kiss.

These regular, non-sexual touches increase oxytocin levels, which enhance feelings of bonding and affection. Daily touch can also reduce stress and anxiety, creating a more relaxed and intimate environment conducive to sexual desire.

Conversation Starters

Use conversation cards or apps designed to prompt deeper discussions. Choose a card during dinner or while relaxing in the evening. Topics can range from personal dreams and desires to sexual fantasies and preferences.

Trying new ways to communicate facilitates communication on topics that might not arise organically, deepening understanding and connection. This practice can open up discussions about sexual needs and desires, making it easier to express and explore them together.

FOR THOSE FLYING SOLO

Mindful Masturbation

Rather than focusing solely on the climax, take time to explore different sensations. Use varying speeds, pressures, and rhythms. Focus on how your body feels during each moment and what sensations bring the most pleasure.

Mindfulness during masturbation increases sexual self-awareness and pleasure, which can boost confidence and satisfaction in solo and partnered sexual activities. It also helps identify what you enjoy, which can be communicated to a partner.

Explore Erotic Literature or Audio

Find erotic books, stories, or audio recordings that appeal to your interests. Schedule regular time to explore these materials, allowing yourself to become immersed in the narratives.

Erotica stimulates the imagination and can increase sexual desire by introducing new fantasies and scenarios. This can also make you more open to exploring different aspects of your sexuality and can enhance solo or partnered experiences by expanding your erotic vocabulary.

Combining Strategies

Both individuals and couples can benefit from a blend of these strategies. For instance, couples might engage in conversation starters that lead to a deeper understanding of each other's fantasies, which can then be explored through scheduled intimacy or daily touch rituals. Individuals can use insights gained from mindful masturbation or erotic literature to enhance their understanding of their desires, which can improve communication and intimacy when in a relationship.

Desire is not static; it shifts and evolves just as we do. By embracing the natural ebb and flow of our desires and the types they take, we can foster a more fulfilling and resilient sexual relationship. Roger and his wife's journey from misunderstanding to a revitalized connection is a testament to the power of communication, understanding, and adaptation in the face of life's inevitable changes.

Through these insights and tools, my hope is that you can navigate the complexities of desire in your own relationships, finding joy and satisfaction in the continual rediscovery of each other's wants and needs.

> **CHAPTER TAKEAWAYS**
>
> - Desire manifests in different ways, including spontaneous and responsive.
> - Navigating mismatched levels of desire requires patience and understanding.
> - Cultivating desire strengthens intimacy and long-term sexual connection.

CHAPTER 9

ARE THERE OTHER PLACES I CAN EXPERIENCE PLEASURE OTHER THAN MY PENIS?

I t's not just your penis . . .
 End of chapter.

Just kidding...

I was speaking with a client of mine the other day. We'll call him Dave. Dave came into our session resistant to talking about involving other parts of his body in sexual play and arousal. Most men I work with have similar outlooks.

On a serious note, arousal, erogenous zones, and sex really are about more than just your penis.

Sex ed, everyone's favorite class growing up, probably taught you that sex is all about your penis and a host of other lies—like your penis will work every time, how to put a condom on, and all the diseases associated with sex.

This conditions you to believe sex is all about your penis, it never takes effort for a man to perform, putting on condoms should be easy (especially after watching your sex ed teacher put one on a banana), and sex can make you physically ill or kill you.

That's a recipe for really bad sexual experiences.

Your expectations aren't properly set up because they're unrealistic and vague. Yes, it's true that the penis is one of the most sensitive parts of the male body and one of the most, if not the most popular, erogenous zones. Still, that doesn't mean you should let it overshadow other parts of your body. They deserve love too.

WHAT IS AN EROGENOUS ZONE?

Male erogenous zones are regions of the male body with heightened sensitivity. They're present across the body and aren't limited to the primary sexual organs. When you stimulate these spots, it can trigger a cascade of pleasure on par with direct sexual contact. Think about it: Do you love having your back scratched, earlobes sucked, or neck kissed? These are some of your erogenous zones in action.

Stimulating erogenous zones feels great because it releases those same feel-good chemicals associated with sexual pleasure and orgasm, like endorphins and oxytocin. If you want to make your partner feel wonderful in more ways than one, learn their favorite erogenous zones and how they want you to touch them. Exploring these areas on your own can also make for some steamy self-love time.

Don't forget that while the whole body is sensitive to sexual touch, individual responses to this stimulation can vary greatly. What feels super arousing to one person might not feel good to another, and that's totally normal. What's important is taking time to discover your preferences and needs as well as those of your partner as you explore each other's bodies.

This isn't a full list, nor is it a list of places you're guaranteed to find sexual pleasure from. In other words, if having your feet touched doesn't get you going, just move on to the next one.

Feet

Many people overlook the sexy potential of feet. I get it. They aren't the greatest things to look at. Still, I'll be the first to tell you they're worth experimenting with. Feet are rich in nerves, and a well-executed foot massage can bring on both relaxation and arousal. Experiment with light touches, gentle pressure, and even toe-sucking if you and your partner really want to go for it.

Belly Button

The belly button is a unique erogenous zone. It's sensitive, often neglected, and responds well to delicate touches and playful circular motions. You can stimulate the belly button with a soft object, like a feather, or introduce edible elements, like flavored oils or sauces. You'll never look at your partner's belly button the same after you lick chocolate, whipped cream, or strawberry sauce out of it.

Just don't try to actually eat it.

Hands and Wrists

Did you know that your hands are packed with nerve endings? Palms and fingers are especially sensitive, and playing with your partner's hands might turn them on. Give them a hand massage and zero in on each finger to help relieve tension and build arousal. Gently stroke and even suck on different parts of their hands to amplify intimacy and tactile stimulation.

Scalp

The scalp responds deeply to gentle touch, which can elicit sexual arousal. Run your fingers or nails softly across your partner's head and press harder if they're OK with it. This relaxing and sexy stimulation is an excellent way to ease into more sensual and intimate encounters.

Backs of the Knees

You may have never thought of this often-overlooked erogenous zone before, but it's surprisingly sensitive to touch. Gentle caresses or kisses behind the knees can send waves of pleasure throughout your partner's body. The skin in this area is very tender, so keep a light touch to amplify the sensation.

Nape of the Neck

The region where the neck meets the hairline is another remarkably delicate area on many men's bodies. This erogenous zone responds well to sensual touch, like light strokes, soft kisses, and even heavy breathing. Add neck stimulation to foreplay or sexual intercourse to enhance the intensity.

Scrotum

The scrotum is located behind your penis and above the perineum, containing your testicles and the lower parts of your spermatic cords. It has plenty of soft, sensitive skin full of nerve endings. It's a key erogenous zone, and many men love it when their partner cups, lightly massages, or gently touches their scrotum. This area is very delicate, so always ask your partner about their preferences for pressure.

Lower Back

Next time you're intimate with your partner, try to focus on their lower back. This area is often full of tension, and a relaxing massage can help relieve stress and prime your partner for sex. Scented lotions can enhance the experience, or you can even find a lube that doubles as a massage oil. Extend the massage to the buttocks and perineum (the space between your anus and genitals) to add an element of sexy surprise.

Inner Thighs

The inner thigh tolerates pressure well, but it's also deeply sensitive. Use varied touches on this erogenous zone, from caressing and light tracing with your nails to deep massaging. Stimulating the inner thighs can be a major turn-on, making it perfect for building anticipation and arousal.

Nipples

While nipples are common for women, they may also offer pleasure for men. If your partner enjoys touch in this area, try tracing their nipples with your fingers, gently kissing them, or softly squeezing them.

Nipple play can amplify sexual pleasure and even lead to orgasm for some people.

Ears

For many people, ear stimulation can fast-track arousal. This is because the earlobes and the skin behind the ears are especially delicate. Try caressing, nibbling, and breathing on your partner's ears to turn them on and get them ready for more action. Soft whispers or gentle kisses around the ears can significantly boost arousal, too.

Genital Area

Try focusing on the entire genital area rather than just the primary sex organs. Explore the area around your partner's pubic bone, including the pubic hairline, and try applying various types of pressure. The area where their belt would rest deserves some attention, too.

Penis

The penis is arguably the most obvious and most popular male erogenous zone. Chances are, your partner knows how they like their penis stimulated, but that doesn't mean you can't explore the tip, shaft, and base in different ways to find what feels good. Try using your hand to make a circle around the base of their penis and squeezing it gently to increase blood flow in the area.

Perineum

The perineum is the area of skin between the scrotum and the anus. It has a rich concentration of nerve endings, making it a great spot to play with. To stimulate this area, apply gentle pressure, lightly flick it, or softly stroke it, especially beneath the testicles. If you and your partner are comfortable with it, explore the perineum's close proximity to the anus—his gateway to prostate stimulation.

LEARN TO ENJOY YOUR ERECTIONS

For this chapter, I want to make sure we highlight the importance of exploring these areas solo as well as with partnered sex. The amount of pleasure gained from these may differ depending on which type you're engaging in, so I want to encourage men to give both a try, experiencing the differences while exploring the similarities.

A lot of guys I work with express various concerns once we get to this stage, almost always honing in on erections. They say things like:

- "If I let myself enjoy this kind of touch, I'll get an erection, and then I'll want to have sex."
- "If I have an erection, my partner might feel pressured to have sex."
- "To get rid of an erection, I have to masturbate."

Getting an erection doesn't mean you need to masturbate or have sex. Yes, exploring your body and sexuality through solo and partnered sex is important, but simply getting an erection doesn't always have to translate into a sexual act.

It goes against the grain, but most guys have never allowed themselves to enjoy an erection without doing anything about it. They're too action-oriented.

You could get an erection, you could not. If you do, can you just enjoy it?

Oftentimes, the messaging that you have to do something with your penis comes when we're young.

A few days ago, I was catching up with a colleague over a video call. She was telling me about her vacation, mentioning an interesting interaction on the return flight that perfectly ties in with this. A boy, no older than 11 or 12, was sitting across the aisle with his mother and sister. Once it was their turn to depart the plane, he turned to her, screaming,

"I CAN'T STAND UP!"

"Why not?" she asked, clearly confused.

He sheepishly pointed to his midsection, where he had an erection he was desperately trying to mask. She told him, point blank, to get rid of it—there wasn't much sympathy from her. My colleague watched empathetically as he tried and failed to make it go away.

The boy's mom went out of her way to make it seem problematic, eventually turning to my friend to apologize for the scene her son created. A scene any boy around that age would've made—because they don't have control of their erections yet.

This interaction is a textbook recipe for shame. It teaches boys at a young age that having an erection is a problem and reinforces the belief that you always have to do something with your penis when aroused, whether that's masturbation or sex.

My goal is to help you understand that having an erection isn't a problem. It's something natural you should enjoy and celebrate about your body.

EROGENOUS ZONES AREN'T JUST FOR SEX

It sounds counterintuitive, but exploring your erogenous zones isn't limited to solo or partnered sex. You don't need to have intercourse or make orgasms the end goal every time. Sometimes, exploring these areas happens because it feels good—and there's nothing wrong with that. At the end of the day, you foster deeper connections between you and your partner.

ARE THERE OTHER PLACES I CAN EXPERIENCE PLEASURE

Scalp
Gentle strokes or light scratching can deeply relax and turn up the heat.

Nape of Neck
Strokes, kisses, or breath here can heighten foreplay.

Hands/Wrists
Loaded with nerve endings; massage, stroke, or kiss to spark arousal.

Lower Back
Massage to release tension; extend to buttocks/perineum for extra spark.

Genital Area
Explore the full region, not just the obvious spots, with varied pressure.

Penis
Tip, shaft, and base all respond differently; explore and vary your touch.

Backs of Knees
Tender skin that loves light caresses or kisses for a surprise thrill.

Ears
Caress, nibble, or whisper to send shivers through the body.

Nipples
Stimulate with touch, kisses, or gentle pressure for amplified pleasure.

Belly Button
Sensitive and often ignored; tease with touch, feathers, or flavored oils.

Scrotum
Soft, nerve-rich skin; cup, massage, or lightly touch (with consent).

Perineum
The nerve-packed bridge between scrotum and anus; gentle pressure or strokes can be intensely pleasurable.

Inner Thighs
Sensitive and receptive to light touches or deep massage to build anticipation.

Feet
Packed with nerves, a foot massage or playful touch can relax and arouse.

To help you kick things off in the right direction, tell your partner where you like to be touched and ask them where they like to be touched.

More often than not, your erogenous zones can also elicit a relaxation or soothing response. Next time you're stressed, anxious, or triggered in conversation with someone, try touching one of these spots (as is socially appropriate). Massage your wrists, touch your neck, etc., to find a place that elicits a calming chemical release and helps you connect to your body.

Time and again, I've been asked the question—What do I do about having a partner who goes straight for my penis?

The simple answer is to communicate directly, outside of sex, that you'd like them to touch you in places other than your penis.

Saying something along the lines of, "*I was thinking, there are other parts of my body that feel really good and bring me sexual pleasure, and I wonder if we can explore those next time we have sex. What other parts of your body bring you pleasure so I can explore?*" goes a long way to show you appreciate having more than your penis stimulated and that you're thinking about your partner at the same time. Who can say no to that?

Bring it up verbally during sex if you prefer that route—just try to find a time that isn't awkward and doesn't completely disrupt the flow between the two of you.

Guiding your partner's hand during sex is another option—show them where you like to be touched.

Sensate focus, which I mentioned briefly in the previous chapter, is an alternative route. It's a form of sexual play focused on enhancing the physical and emotional connection you share with your partner through touch and communication. You focus more on sensory perceptions (anything you perceive with your five senses) and sensuality instead of each other's genitals and penetrative sex. I've seen it help couples become more present in their relationships, especially during sex, leading to a more satisfying sexual relationship.

So, remember—there's more to a fulfilling sex life than your penis. Explore the various erogenous zones on your own and with your partner. Who knows, you may end up finding a new favorite outside of your penis.

CHAPTER TAKEAWAYS

- Pleasure extends beyond penetration, with various erogenous zones enhancing experience.
- Exploring new types of touch deepens intimacy and personal enjoyment.
- Communicating preferences opens doors to richer and more varied sensations.

PART 2

Demystifying Partnered Sex

CHAPTER 10

WHAT MAKES A SEXUAL RELATIONSHIP HEALTHY?

When I say partnered sex, people typically think one of two things. One group thinks about any sexual partner, and the other group thinks about a long-term monogamous commitment between two people.

In this chapter I aim to give insight into all of the different ways sexual partners relate without judgment or criticism. I want this to be a chapter you can refer to for definitions and some helpful tips for navigating each type of partnership.

To start, let me tell you about Jim. Jim came into my office with a heavy heart. His friends had been criticizing him for engaging in casual sex, suggesting that he should focus on settling down.

"I've been feeling a lot of pressure from my friends lately. They keep telling me I should settle down and find a long-term partner."

"And how does that make you feel, Jim?"

"Confused, mostly. I enjoy the casual relationships I have, but part of me wonders if they're right. Maybe I'm just avoiding commitment. Maybe I need to grow up."

"What do you enjoy about your current relationships?"

"I like the freedom and the lack of pressure. I can connect with different people without the expectations of a long-term commitment."

"And do you feel fulfilled by these relationships?"

"For the most part, yes. But sometimes I wonder if I'm missing out on something more meaningful."

"It's natural to question and evaluate your relationships. There's no one right way to connect with others. The key is to find what works for you and makes you happy."

"But what about the long-term? Am I setting myself up for failure by not settling down?"

"Not necessarily. Many people find fulfillment in different types of relationships throughout their lives. What matters most is clear communication, mutual consent, and that you feel your needs are being met."

"But everyone else seems to be settling down. I feel like I should want to."

Jim's experience is a common one, highlighting societal pressures that often pathologize having multiple sexual partners. It's important to remember that all sexual relationships are valid as long as there is clear communication and consent.

TYPES OF CASUAL SEXUAL RELATIONSHIPS

Casual Sex

Casual sex refers to sexual activity between individuals without the expectation of a romantic relationship or social interaction beyond the sexual encounter. This could be a one-time hookup, an occasional meeting, or a regular arrangement. I've worked with clients who have casual sex arrangements with multiple people in cities they travel to, and others who enjoy casual hookups and one-night stands.

Society will often try to convince you that these arrangements are somehow less enlightened than long-term commitments, but that simply isn't true. The right sexual relationship for you is one that works in the life you have now and helps support the person you want to become. That might mean you meet and marry someone in college, but it might also mean you enjoy time with different people, in different zip codes, for different lengths of time.

Casual sex is only a problem when consent and communication aren't on point.

Things to Consider:

- If casual sex is your go-to partnered-sex activity, you'll probably encounter some judgment. Be careful who you share with and move on; as long as you're comfortable with your decisions, it's no one else's business.
- Consent matters. I'm not just talking about consent for sexual contact—that is, of course, paramount. But, when you're engaging in casual sex you have to ask your partners to consent to exactly what you're looking for. If you want a one-night stand, say that. If you want an every Friday night hook-up, make that clear. Contrary to what others might say, being this clear is kind and allows the other party the opportunity to consider if this is what they want or not.
- Studies have found that casual sex is not correlated with higher rates of sexually transmitted infections as long as you engage in safe sex practices (which brings me to my next point).[25]
- Communicate about everything. When you're having casual sex with someone, the very premise is that you don't know them well. Asking questions every step of the way will help ensure you both have a good time. Ask what they're into, what they want out of the sexual experience, and tell them what you like as well. You'll also want to communicate about things like safe-sex practices, and how often you want to see one another.

---

[25] Wang, K., Chen, S., & Wu, F. (2023). Dating app use and sexual risk: Understanding the associations between casual sex motivation, number of sexual partners, and STI diagnoses. *International Journal of Sexual Health, 35*(2), 209–217. https://doi.org/10.1080/19317611.2023.2184898.

Characteristics of Casual Sexual Relationships

- **No Friendship Component:** Casual sex partners typically do not have a friendship; the relationship is purely sexual.
- **Simplicity:** The focus is solely on sexual gratification without the complexities of an emotional bond.

Friends with Benefits (FWB)

A friends with benefits relationship involves two consenting adults who engage in a primarily sexual relationship *without* the commitment of a romantic partnership. They might spend time together as friends, go out on dates, or simply hook up on a semi-regular basis. The key is that the relationship does not have a long-term commitment goal. These relationships may or may not be monogamous.

Important Considerations for FWB

- **Consent and Clarity:** Both parties must consent to the nature of the relationship and clearly communicate their wants, needs, and boundaries. If you're looking for a FWB relationship, you need to be clear about that from the start. Often, a FWB relationship morphs out of a casual sex arrangement, but not always. Regardless, frequent, clear discussions are necessary.[26]
- **Regular Check-Ins:** It's helpful to have regular, non-sexual check-ins to discuss where both individuals stand emotionally and sexually. It's tough to have regular physical sex contact with someone and not develop some fondness and emotional connection. An emotional connection, though, does not mean

---

[26] Beres, M. (2009). Sexual miscommunication? Untangling assumptions about sexual communication between casual sex partners. *Culture, Health & Sexuality, 12*(1), 1–14. https://doi.org/10.1080/13691050903075226.

your arrangement needs to become a committed relationship. Having feelings and acting on them are two different things.
- **Flexibility:** These relationships can evolve. Some might end, while others could develop into more serious relationships, but this should be communicated openly.[27]

Jim's Dilemma

Jim struggled with societal expectations that deem casual sex as immature or unhealthy. Society often views casual sex as inferior to committed relationships, suggesting it as a stepping stone to a "right" relationship. However, the truth is that various types of relationships can be fulfilling. It's critical to find the one that works for you at your current stage of life and be honest about whether your needs are being met.

MONOGAMOUS RELATIONSHIPS

Let's talk a little bit about monogamous relationships. If you're choosing to invest emotionally and sexually in only one partner, you're likely opting for a bond that feels both stable and safe. Societal and cultural norms often reinforce monogamy, so it may feel like the most familiar or "default" relationship structure.[28] The truth is that monogamy is rare both in nature and in human relationships.[29] Different relationship

---

[27] Farvid, P., & Braun, V. (2016). Unpacking the "pleasures" and "pains" of heterosexual casual sex: Beyond singular understandings. *The Journal of Sex Research*, 54(1), 73–90. https://doi.org/10.1080/00224499.2016.1143442.

[28] Solomon, N. G., & Ophir, A. G. (2020). What's love got to do with it: The evolution of monogamy. *Frontiers in Ecology and Evolution*, 8, 110. https://doi.org/10.3389/fevo.2020.00110.

[29] Schacht, R., & Kramer, K. L. (2019). Are we monogamous? A review of the evolution of pair-bonding in humans and its contemporary variation cross-culturally. *Frontiers in Ecology and Evolution*, 7, 230. https://doi.org/10.3389/fevo.2019.00230.

structures exist across the globe, but the most common type is serial monogamy, where a person might pair with several people throughout a lifetime, but typically only one at any given moment.[30]

But it's crucial to remember that a monogamous relationship doesn't magically take care of itself—intentionality is key.

Here are a few things I always tell my clients to keep in mind:

- **Exclusivity:** All emotional and sexual needs are met within this relationship. While this can foster deep trust and connection, it also means both partners need to remain attuned to each other's changing desires over time.
- **Shared Responsibilities:** Managing finances, household tasks, and parenting can create a sense of teamwork, but also lead to stress if one partner feels overburdened. Regular communication about who does what helps keep the relationship fair and balanced.
- **Prioritization:** Between work, kids, and everyday demands, it's easy to let sexual intimacy take a back seat. Scheduling intentional time for each other—whether it's date nights, weekend getaways, or just open, honest conversations—can help you stay connected.
- **Defining Monogamy:** Every couple has a unique perspective on what's acceptable. For some, flirting might be off-limits, while others are comfortable with it. Porn use, interactions on social media, and even friendships with someone of the opposite sex can spark conflict if boundaries aren't clearly discussed in advance. It's essential to talk openly about these gray areas so everyone feels respected and secure.

Ultimately, monogamy can be incredibly rewarding when you both feel safe enough to share your vulnerabilities and desires. By checking

---

[30] Schacht, R., & Kramer, K. L. (2019). Are we monogamous? A review of the evolution of pair-bonding in humans and its contemporary variation cross-culturally. *Frontiers in Ecology and Evolution, 7*, 230. https://doi.org/10.3389/fevo.2019.00230.

in regularly, clarifying expectations, and being open to adjusting course when needed, you'll foster a healthy, satisfying dynamic that can stand the test of time.

A Couple's Journey

A couple came to see me because they were struggling with communication in their monogamous relationship. The wife felt disrespected by her husband's porn use and the way he looked at other women. They had never defined their boundaries clearly, leading to misunderstandings and hurt feelings. By normalizing attraction and discussing their expectations, they could better navigate their monogamous agreement.

John and Lisa's Story

John and Lisa had been married for ten years and had always considered themselves to be in a happy, monogamous relationship. However, over time, they noticed that the excitement and passion in their sex life had diminished. John felt that Lisa was no longer interested in sex, while Lisa felt that John was not making enough effort to be romantic. This misunderstanding led to feelings of neglect and frustration on both sides.

They decided to seek therapy to address their issues. Through open communication and exercises aimed at rebuilding intimacy, they rediscovered their connection. They learned the importance of expressing their desires and concerns openly and found new ways to prioritize their sexual relationship. This renewed focus on their sexual connection helped reignite the passion in their marriage, leading to a deeper emotional bond.

CONSENSUAL NON-MONOGAMY (CNM)

Just mentioning non-monogamy in a group setting will have some people clucking their tongues, others rolling their eyes, and some spitting out insults. Despite the way many monogamous people view non-monogamy, non-monogamous couples, throuples, and so on report high levels of relationship satisfaction.[31] Consensual non-monogamy includes various forms of relationships where individuals have emotional and/or sexual relationships with more than one person. This can include polyamory, open relationships, and swinging.

Characteristics:

- Communication: Clear communication about boundaries, rules, and expectations is crucial.
- Written Agreements: Documenting agreements can prevent misunderstandings.
- Flexibility: These relationships can vary widely, with each connection being unique.

Polyamorous Relationships

Polyamory involves engaging in multiple romantic and sexual relationships simultaneously, with the knowledge and consent of everyone involved. These relationships can be complex and require a high level of communication and emotional intelligence.

Characteristics:

- Multiple Relationships: Individuals may have several committed relationships simultaneously.
- Honesty and Transparency: Open communication about feelings, expectations, and boundaries is essential.

---

[31] Rodrigues, D. L. (2024). A narrative review of the dichotomy between the social views of non-monogamy and the experiences of consensual non-monogamous people. *Archives of Sexual Behavior, 53*(3), 931–940. https://doi.org/10.1007/s10508-023-02786-1.

- Compersion: This is the feeling of joy one gets from seeing their partner happy with someone else. It contrasts with jealousy and is often a goal in polyamorous relationships.

Sara and David's Story

Sara and David had been together for five years when they realized that their emotional and sexual needs were not fully met within the confines of a monogamous relationship. They decided to explore polyamory, which allowed them to pursue additional relationships while maintaining their bond.

Initially, they faced challenges with jealousy and insecurity, but through continuous open dialogue and setting clear boundaries, they navigated these emotions. They learned to practice compersion, finding happiness in each other's connections with other partners. Over time, their primary relationship strengthened, and they both felt more fulfilled.

Open Relationships

Open relationships allow partners to engage in sexual activities with others outside the primary relationship. Unlike polyamory, open relationships typically focus more on sexual rather than romantic connections with others.

Characteristics:

- Primary Partnership: There is usually a primary, committed relationship that takes precedence.
- Sexual Freedom: Partners have the freedom to explore sexual activities with others.
- Rules and Boundaries: Establishing rules about safe sex, emotional involvement, and disclosure is crucial.

Chris and Emma's Story

Chris and Emma had been married for twelve years and were deeply committed to each other. However, they found that their sexual desires had evolved and were interested in exploring new experiences. They decided to open their relationship, allowing each other to have sexual encounters with other people.

To ensure their relationship remained strong, they set clear rules: always practice safe sex, avoid developing emotional attachments with outside partners, and share their experiences with each other. This openness added excitement to their relationship and deepened their trust and communication. They found that exploring their sexual interests outside their marriage brought them closer together.

Swinging

Swingers are committed couples who consensually engage in extra-relational sex for recreational purposes. There's not a ton of research on the swinging community because of the social stigma participants fear. However, a study that interviewed thirty-two swingers evaluated marital satisfaction and found that as long as they prioritized effective communication, there was an increase in how positively they rated their relationship.[32]

Just like with any relationship structure, there are different types of swinging relationships. Here's an overview.

---

[32] Kimberly, C., & Hans, J. D. (2017). From fantasy to reality: A grounded theory of experiences in the swinging lifestyle. *Archives of Sexual Behavior, 46*(3), 789–799. https://doi.org/10.1007/s10508-015-0621-2.

Soft Swap

- Couples engage in sexual activities with others up to a certain limit (e.g., kissing, touching, oral sex) but typically do not include intercourse with partners outside the relationship.
- Often considered a "lighter" or introductory form of swinging.

Full Swap

- Couples consent to their partner engaging in all forms of sexual activity, including intercourse, with other individuals.
- Requires clear boundaries and open communication to maintain comfort levels for all involved.

Same-Room vs. Separate-Room

- Same-Room: All participants share one room, allowing partners to see and interact with their own partner as well as others.
- Separate-Room: Partners may engage with others in different rooms, sometimes preferred if individuals are more comfortable with private experiences.

Voyeurs

- Individuals or couples who enjoy watching others engage in sexual activity without directly participating.
- Voyeurism can be part of an event or private arrangement and may serve as a precursor to more active involvement.

Exhibitionists

- They enjoy being watched by others while engaged in sexual activity.

- This may take place in group settings, clubs, parties, or private gatherings where observers are welcome.

Group Encounters

- This can involve multiple couples or a mix of singles and couples participating together.
- The level of interaction ranges from soft swap in a group setting to full swapping with multiple partners.

Single Participants (a.k.a. "Lifestyle Singles")

- While "swinging" is often associated with couples, single individuals (both men and women) participate and identify as part of the lifestyle.
- They may engage as additional partners to couples, join group activities, or date other singles within the community.

Variations in Emotional Involvement

- Some participants focus on purely recreational or physical aspects, while others form close friendships or "friends-with-benefits" type connections.
- Regardless of emotional involvement, clear boundaries and communication remain crucial.

Consent and communication lie at the heart of every healthy romantic partnership, regardless of its structure or dynamics. In swinging relationships, these elements become all the more critical. Ensuring explicit, ongoing consent from all involved fosters trust and respect, just as it would in any monogamous or polyamorous context. Regular check-ins, honest discussions, and clearly defined boundaries allow everyone to feel heard and secure. By prioritizing open dialogue, couples (and singles) can maintain a sense of mutual comfort and navigate any challenges that arise—ultimately strengthening their connection and enhancing their overall satisfaction.

THE BOTTOM LINE ABOUT PARTNERED SEX

All sexual relationships can be valid and fulfilling as long as they are based on clear communication, mutual consent, and respect. Whether it's casual sex, friends with benefits, monogamy, or consensual non-monogamy, the key is to find what works best for you and your partner(s) at any given stage in life. Understanding and respecting the diversity of sexual relationships is crucial for personal growth and satisfaction.

By recognizing and embracing the variety of ways people can connect, we create a more inclusive and accepting view of human sexuality. Remember, the most important aspect of any relationship is that it meets the needs of those involved and that all parties feel respected and fulfilled.

CHAPTER TAKEAWAYS

- Healthy sexual relationships are based on mutual respect, communication, and pleasure.
- Defining personal values and expectations creates a foundation for fulfillment.
- Prioritizing connection over performance fosters deeper intimacy.

CHAPTER 11

HOW DO I TALK TO MY PARTNER ABOUT SEX WITHOUT IT BEING AWKWARD?

It's no accident that I put a chapter on communication right after a chapter where I discussed different types of relationship structures. Sex is an integral part of most intimate relationships, yet it can often become a source of discomfort and tension when communication about it falters. Many couples, like Dan and Erin, find themselves struggling with their sexual connection after years of avoiding direct conversations about their needs, desires, and frustrations. Dan felt bored and disinterested, while Erin felt confused and worried. Neither had initiated a conversation about their sex life in over 15 years, operating under the assumption that they knew everything about each other. This lack of communication led to misunderstandings and unmet needs, causing a rift in their intimacy.

"Honestly, we just . . . assumed we knew everything about each other. We've been married for fifteen years and have known each other for twenty-five years. It felt like there wasn't much more to talk about, you know?"

"We've been together for so long, it's like we thought we didn't need to have these conversations. I guess we just figured that if something was really wrong, the other person would bring it up. But neither of us did."

We don't intrinsically know how to talk about sex with our partners because many of us aren't raised talking about sex at all. Sex education happens in a classroom and is mostly about procreation or the prevention of diseases. The connection piece is missing entirely so it's no wonder so many couples wind up in a situation where they can't figure out exactly what's wrong with their sex life but are ill equipped to even begin a conversation about it.

In therapy with Dan and Erin, we started with a conversation about their most recent sexual experience (this is one of my favorite ways to open with a couple). During that conversation it became clear that the usual way of doing things wasn't working for Erin.

"It just feels like we do the same thing every time, and that night wasn't any different. Sure, it was nice to connect, but I didn't get the intensity I was craving. I haven't for a while."

Dan's response, if he weren't sitting in a therapist's office, might have been to talk about the fact that she hadn't complained or that she did in fact orgasm, but, lucky for them both, I was there to guide the conversation.

Eventually, we found out that the same old same old wasn't working for Dan either.

"I've stopped initiating as often because I know what the experience is going to be. Is it enjoyable? Yeah. Is it exciting? Not always."

If you're paying attention, as I was, it becomes clear that they both want excitement. Their goal as a couple is aligned, they just haven't talked about sex enough to realize that. Once they realized they wanted the same thing out of their sex life, we could begin the work of detailing what, exactly, they wanted to try to make things more exciting. Common ground comes first, then exploration can follow.

UNDERSTANDING THE DISCOMFORT

Talking about sex can be incredibly uncomfortable, even with a partner you've known for years. The discomfort often stems from societal taboos, personal insecurities, and the vulnerability required to discuss such an intimate topic. Unlike other subjects, we aren't typically equipped with the tools or language to navigate these conversations effectively. As a result, many couples avoid them altogether, hoping the issues will resolve themselves. Unfortunately, this rarely happens.

To move past this discomfort, it's essential to acknowledge that discussing sex is inherently challenging. If you wait until you feel comfortable bringing it up, the conversation may never happen. Similarly, if you wait for your partner to initiate the discussion, you might be waiting indefinitely. The key is to lean into the vulnerability and recognize that the discomfort is a natural part of the process.

THE IMPORTANCE OF VULNERABILITY

When approaching a difficult conversation about sex, it's helpful to draw parallels to other challenging topics you might discuss with your partner. Consider, for instance, the anxiety that comes with discussing financial difficulties, such as losing a job or needing to cut back on expenses. These conversations are uncomfortable, and there's never a "perfect" time to have them. However, moving through the discomfort is necessary for resolving the issue.

Talking about sex is similar. The discomfort arises from the significant meaning we attach to sex, just as we do with money. You might worry that discussing your sexual needs or concerns will change the dynamics of your relationship. Questions like "Will they still be attracted to me?" or "Will this make things weird between us?" can fuel anxiety and prevent you from initiating the conversation. However, just as with financial discussions, addressing the issue head-on is the only way to move forward.

INITIATING THE CONVERSATION

When you're ready to talk about sex, it's important to approach the conversation thoughtfully. Start by expressing your concerns and acknowledging the difficulty of the topic. You might say something like:

"I have a difficult topic I need to bring up. I'm worried about talking with you and might not have all the right words. I need your patience and help getting through this conversation. Can you do that for me? Is now a good time?"

This approach does several things: it sets the stage for a supportive dialogue, acknowledges the vulnerability involved, and seeks consent from your partner to engage in the conversation. Gaining consent is crucial because it ensures that both of you are mentally and emotionally prepared to discuss such a sensitive topic.

Saying the Hard Thing

Once you've established a supportive environment, it's time to "say the thing" that's been on your mind. Whether it's expressing dissatisfaction with your sex life, a desire to explore new activities like BDSM, or feelings of boredom, it's important to be direct and honest. After you've said your piece, give your partner space to respond. This is where many people falter—out of anxiety, they might start rambling to fill the silence or try to rationalize their feelings.

Resist the urge to fill the silence. Allow your partner time to process what you've said and respond. If they don't immediately have a response, gently prompt them by asking, "What is coming up for you? I just said something difficult. What is your reaction? Is there anything I could help clarify?"

HANDLING DIFFERENT TYPES OF SEXUAL CONVERSATIONS

Sexual conversations can vary greatly depending on the topic, and each requires a different approach to ensure that both partners feel heard, respected, and understood. Below are strategies for handling specific types of sexual conversations, including "I'm not satisfied," "I'd like to try something new," "I was wondering about," and "I'm struggling with."

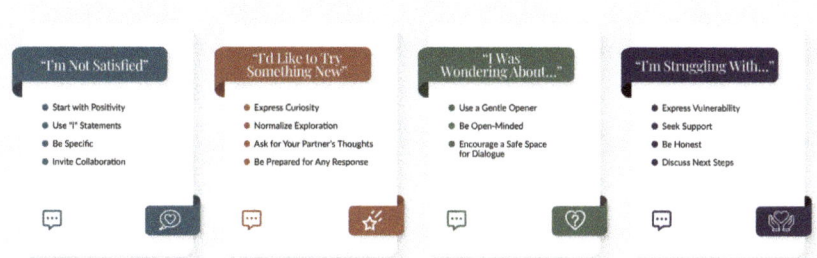

"I'm Not Satisfied"

This conversation is perhaps one of the most difficult to initiate, as it touches on feelings of inadequacy, rejection, and vulnerability. However, it is crucial for maintaining a healthy sexual relationship.

Approach:

- **Start with Positivity:** Begin the conversation by expressing what you appreciate about your sexual relationship. Acknowledge the things that do work well, which can help soften the impact of discussing dissatisfaction.
- **Use "I" Statements:** Frame your concerns from your perspective to avoid sounding accusatory. For example, "I feel like our sex life isn't as fulfilling as it used to be for me."
- **Be Specific:** Clearly articulate what aspects of your sex life aren't satisfying. Is it the frequency, the type of activities, the level of intimacy? The more specific you are, the better your partner will understand your concerns.
- **Invite Collaboration:** Suggest working together to improve your sexual relationship. For example, "I'd love for us to explore ways we can both feel more fulfilled."

Example Script: "I've been thinking about our sex life, and while there are many things I love about it, I've been feeling that I'm not as satisfied as I'd like to be. I think we could benefit from talking about what we both need to feel more connected and fulfilled. Would you be open to discussing this with me?"

"I'd Like to Try Something New"

Introducing new elements into your sexual relationship can be exciting, but it can also bring up fears of rejection or discomfort. It's important to approach this conversation with openness and curiosity.

Approach:

- **Express Curiosity:** Frame your desire as an exploration rather than a demand. Show that you're curious and open to discovering new experiences together.
- **Normalize Exploration:** Reinforce that it's normal and healthy for couples to want to try new things and that this curiosity is a sign of growth in your relationship.
- **Ask for Your Partner's Thoughts:** After sharing your idea, ask your partner how they feel about it. Be open to their response, whether it's positive or hesitant.
- **Be Prepared for Any Response:** Understand that your partner might not be immediately enthusiastic, and be ready to have a patient, non-judgmental discussion.

Example Script: "I've been thinking about our sex life, and I'd like to explore something new together. I think it could be really fun and bring us even closer. What do you think about trying [specific activity]? I'm curious to hear your thoughts and whether this is something you'd be interested in."

"I Was Wondering About . . ."

This phrase is often used to introduce a question or curiosity about something you've been thinking about, whether it's related to fantasies, desires, or understanding your partner's preferences.

Approach:

- **Use a Gentle Opener:** Begin with a soft introduction to ensure your partner feels comfortable. This approach helps to ease into the topic without overwhelming them.
- **Be Open-Minded:** Show that you're open to whatever your partner's response might be, whether they share your curiosity or not.
- **Encourage a Safe Space for Dialogue:** Make it clear that you're bringing this up because you want to understand each other better, not because you expect anything specific.

Example Script: "I was wondering about something, and I wanted to get your thoughts. Have you ever thought about [fantasy, activity, etc.]? I'm curious to know how you feel about it or if it's something you've ever been interested in."

"I'm Struggling With . . ."

Discussing personal struggles related to sex, such as performance anxiety, low libido, or emotional disconnect, can be challenging due to the vulnerability involved. However, sharing these struggles is essential for building a supportive and understanding relationship.

Approach:

- **Express Vulnerability:** Acknowledge that it's difficult for you to bring this up, which can help your partner understand the seriousness and sensitivity of the issue.

- **Seek Support:** Frame the conversation as a way to seek your partner's support rather than just to inform them of a problem. This helps create a team-oriented approach to the issue.
- **Be Honest:** Share your feelings openly and try to articulate what's been difficult for you. Whether it's a physical issue, an emotional barrier, or something else, honesty is key.
- **Discuss Next Steps:** After sharing your struggle, talk about how you can work together to address it. This could involve seeking professional help, trying different approaches, or simply being more patient with each other.

Example Script: "I've been struggling with something in our sex life, and I've been hesitant to bring it up because it's really difficult for me. Lately, I've been feeling [describe the issue], and I'm not sure what to do about it. I really need your support as we figure this out together. Can we talk about how we might approach this?"

HANDLING DIFFERENT RESPONSES

In an ideal world, your partner would respond with empathy and a willingness to engage in a constructive conversation. However, we don't live in a perfect world, and it's important to be prepared for different types of responses.

Unsupportive Responses

If your partner reacts negatively, it's crucial to remember that their response reflects their own feelings and insecurities, not the validity of your concerns. If their response includes violent or intentionally hurtful language, you have the right to pause the conversation. You might say, "That response is not helpful. I'm going to end the conversation here. Let me know when we can talk about this again."

In some cases, the conversation might need the guidance of a therapist or coach, especially if it becomes clear that productive communication is difficult to achieve on your own.

Supportive Responses

On the other hand, if your partner responds with curiosity and questions, that's a positive sign. Engage in a dialogue that explores both of your positions, seeks common ground, and looks for solutions that satisfy both of your needs. This type of conversation can significantly deepen your intimacy and understanding of each other.

THE ROLE OF CONTINUOUS COMMUNICATION

One important takeaway from Dan and Erin's experience is that communication about sex should not be a one-time event. It needs to be an ongoing dialogue that evolves as your relationship does. Regular check-ins about your sexual relationship can prevent misunderstandings and keep both partners satisfied and connected.

CONVERSATION PLANNER FOR COUPLES

To facilitate these conversations, couples can use the following conversation planner to prepare and guide their discussions about sensitive topics, including sex.

Conversation Planner

1. **Identify the Issue:**
    - What specific concern or desire do you want to discuss?
    - Why is this important to you?

2. **Assess Your Readiness:**
   - Are you emotionally prepared to discuss this topic?
   - Have you considered how your partner might react?
   - Are you ready to listen to your partner's perspective without judgment?
3. **Choose the Right Time:**
   - Is this a good time for both of you to talk?
   - Are there any potential distractions that could be minimized?
4. **Set the Tone:**
   - Start by expressing your love and commitment to the relationship.
   - Acknowledge the difficulty of the conversation.
   - Ask for your partner's support and patience.
5. **State the Issue Clearly:**
   - Be direct and specific about what you want to discuss.
   - Use "I" statements to express your feelings and concerns.
6. **Pause and Listen:**
   - After stating your concerns, pause to let your partner respond.
   - Resist the urge to fill the silence or defend your position immediately.
7. **Encourage Dialogue:**
   - Ask open-ended questions to understand your partner's feelings.
   - Discuss potential solutions together.
8. **Agree on Next Steps:**
   - Summarize what was discussed.
   - Agree on any actions or changes you both are willing to make.
   - Set a time to check in on the progress.
9. **Reflect and Reassess:**
   - After the conversation, reflect on how it went.
   - Consider what went well and what could be improved for future discussions.

HOW DO I TALK TO MY PARTNER ABOUT SEX 155

CHAPTER TAKEAWAYS

- Open conversations about sex strengthen relationships and eliminate misunderstandings.
- Expressing desires and boundaries clearly enhances trust and connection.
- Emotional connection matters as much as technique for satisfying intimacy.

CHAPTER 12

WHAT'S THE POINT OF PARTNERED SEX?

When couples come to see me, it's often because they've forgotten the point of partnered sex. Over time, life's demands and the complexities of relationships can obscure what once felt so natural and fulfilling. This was the case for John and Claire, who hadn't had intercourse for over 10 years when they first walked into my office. Their lack of sexual connection had become a source of tension, leading to miscommunication and hurt feelings. However, the real issue wasn't just about sex itself—it was about losing sight of what partnered sex truly means.

THE MISCONCEPTION: INTERCOURSE AS THE ULTIMATE GOAL

When John and Claire began their sessions, their focus was almost entirely on the absence of intercourse in their relationship. To them, the solution seemed simple: if they could just start having intercourse again, everything would fall into place. They expressed frustration when I tried to steer the conversation toward intimacy, connection, and foreplay. For them, these aspects felt like distractions from the "real" issue—the lack of intercourse.

This narrow focus on intercourse isn't uncommon. Many couples believe that intercourse is the pinnacle of sexual activity and that everything else is secondary. However, this mindset can lead to overlooking the broader aspects of sexual connection that are crucial for a fulfilling relationship.

SHIFTING THE FOCUS: CONNECTION OVER LOGISTICS

To help John and Claire, I first needed to shift their perspective. I asked them to take a step back and reflect on how their relationship began. I asked them questions like:

- How did you meet?
- What was that like? How did it feel?
- How did you know you were interested in your partner? What stood out to you?
- Describe some of your early sexual experiences together.

These questions were designed to reconnect them with the emotional and physical connection they once had, beyond just the act of intercourse. Early in their relationship, sex wasn't just about logistics like touch, orgasm, or favorite positions—it was about play, discovery, and connection. Sex felt exciting, low-stakes, and full of joy. It was an expression of their bond, not just a series of physical acts.

THE IMPORTANCE OF PLAY IN ADULT RELATIONSHIPS

Adults need play just as much as children do, though we often forget this as we grow older. Play isn't just about having fun—it's a crucial part of human interaction that fosters creativity, connection, and joy.[33] In the context of a sexual relationship, playfulness can reignite the passion and intimacy that might have faded over time.

---

[33] Baumeister, R. F., & Vohs, K. D. (2021). Sexual motivation, evolution, and the nature of desire. *Social and Personality Psychology Compass, 15*(6), e12589. https://doi.org/10.1111/spc3.12589.

When I explained this to John and Claire, they were initially skeptical. Their focus had been so narrow for so long that it was difficult for them to see how something as seemingly unrelated as play could improve their sex life. However, as we explored this concept further, they began to understand that sex wasn't just about the act of intercourse—it was about enjoying each other's company, being present in the moment, and allowing themselves to be vulnerable and open.

REDISCOVERING CONNECTION THROUGH TOUCH

One of the first steps in rekindling their sexual connection was to reintroduce non-sexual touch into their relationship. For John and Claire, touch had become something that only led to sex, which created pressure and anxiety around it. They had stopped touching each other in affectionate, non-sexual ways, which only reinforced the distance between them.

I suggested that they start by simply lying in bed together and cuddling without any expectation of it leading to sex. This exercise wasn't about initiating intercourse; it was about rediscovering the comfort and connection that comes from physical closeness. Over time, as they became more comfortable with touch, they found that they were laughing more, feeling more relaxed, and experiencing a deeper sense of connection.

FROM CONNECTION TO INTERCOURSE: A GRADUAL PROCESS

As John and Claire's connection grew, they found that they could finally talk about intercourse in a more helpful and less pressured way. They realized that the key to rekindling their sexual relationship wasn't to force intercourse but to rebuild the intimacy and trust that had been missing for so long. With this new foundation, they were able to approach intercourse as a natural extension of their growing closeness, rather than as a goal that had to be achieved at all costs.

In one of our sessions, John admitted, "I hate to admit this, but I really enjoy some of this other stuff as much as I enjoy intercourse." Claire turned to him with a smile and said, "Me too!" This was a breakthrough moment for them—they realized that by taking a step back from their fixation on intercourse, they could reimagine what sex looked like in their relationship. It became less about logistics and more about enjoying the experience together.

THE ROLE OF COMMUNICATION

One of the biggest challenges for John and Claire was communication. Their years of miscommunication had created a cycle of frustration and hurt feelings. They often talked past each other, with neither fully understanding what the other was trying to convey. This was particularly true when it came to discussing their sex life.

To break this cycle, we worked on improving their communication skills. I encouraged them to be more open and honest about their needs and desires, but also to listen actively to each other without judgment. One of the exercises I recommended was for each of them to write down their thoughts about their relationship and sex life, then exchange their writings and read them aloud to each other. This helped them communicate more clearly and reduce the chances of misunderstanding or making assumptions about what the other person meant.

Here's an outline of the questions I had them answer and share with each other to move further:

- Describe your sexual experience with your partner over the last year.
- What aspects of those two descriptions do you want to have in your sex life now?
- What's one thing you can add in right now?

This exercise helped John and Claire reconnect with the positive aspects of their relationship and reminded them of what they valued about each other. By focusing on the emotional and physical connection they had built over the years, they were able to approach their sexual relationship with a renewed sense of purpose and joy.

UNDERSTANDING THE BROADER PURPOSE OF PARTNERED SEX

So, what is the point of partnered sex? It's a question that many couples lose sight of as they become bogged down by the logistics of sex—positions, frequency, and performance. But the true purpose of partnered sex goes far beyond these technicalities. Partnered sex is about connection, intimacy, and the shared experience of pleasure and play. It's about creating a bond that goes deeper than physical satisfaction, fostering a sense of closeness and trust that can enhance every aspect of the relationship.

THE SHIFT FROM INTERCOURSE-FOCUSED TO CONNECTION-FOCUSED

One of the most important shifts that John and Claire made was moving from an intercourse-focused mindset to a connection-focused one. They realized that while intercourse is an important part of a sexual relationship, it's not the only part. By broadening their understanding of what sex could be, they opened themselves up to a richer, more fulfilling sexual experience.

This shift allowed them to rediscover the joy of playfulness in their relationship. They began to explore new ways of being intimate with each other, without the pressure of it always leading to intercourse. They experimented with different types of touch, engaged in more extended foreplay, and even found new activities that brought them closer together, like dancing or taking baths together.

One of the most significant outcomes of John and Claire's journey was their ability to reimagine what partnered sex could look like. By stepping back from their previous focus on intercourse and orgasm, they were able to see sex as a broader experience that included connection, intimacy, and play.

They learned that sex didn't have to fit a specific script to be satisfying. It could be messy, imperfect, and still incredibly fulfilling. By letting go of their preconceived notions about what sex should be, they opened themselves up to new possibilities and a deeper connection with each other.

PRACTICAL STEPS FOR COUPLES

If you and your partner find yourselves in a similar situation, here are some practical steps to help you rediscover the point of partnered sex:

1. **Reflect on Your Relationship:** Take time to reflect on how your relationship began and what made you fall in love with your partner. What were your early sexual experiences like? What has changed since then, and what do you miss?
2. **Reintroduce Non-Sexual Touch:** Start by incorporating non-sexual touch into your daily routine. This could be as simple as holding hands, cuddling, or giving each other a massage. The goal is to rebuild physical connection without the immediate expectation of sex.
3. **Focus on Play:** Find ways to bring playfulness back into your relationship. This could involve trying new activities together, exploring fantasies, or just being silly with each other. Remember, play is about enjoying each other's company without pressure.
4. **Communicate Openly:** Work on improving your communication around sex. This includes being honest about your needs

and desires but also being a good listener when your partner shares theirs. Consider using writing exercises to clarify your thoughts and share them with each other.
5. **Redefine Sex:** Broaden your definition of what sex means in your relationship. Instead of focusing solely on intercourse, explore other ways of being intimate, whether that's through touch, oral sex, or simply spending time naked together. And remember, this definition is never fixed; you and/or your partner(s) can redefine it at any time.
6. **Embrace Imperfection:** Let go of the idea that sex has to be perfect or follow a specific script. Allow yourselves to be vulnerable and experiment without fear of failure. The goal is to enjoy the experience together, whatever form it takes.

John and Claire's story illustrates how easy it is to lose sight of the broader purpose of partnered sex. When couples focus too much on the logistics—positions, orgasms, frequency—they can miss out on the deeper connection that sex is meant to foster. By rediscovering the joy of play, improving their communication, and broadening their definition of sex, John and Claire were able to rebuild their intimacy and find a renewed sense of closeness in their relationship.

The point of partnered sex isn't just about physical satisfaction—it's about connection, intimacy, and shared experiences that bring you closer together. It's about enjoying each other's company, being present in the moment, and allowing yourselves to be vulnerable and open. When you focus on these aspects, sex becomes more than just an act—it becomes a vital part of your relationship that strengthens your bond and enhances your overall well-being.

As you move forward in your relationship, remember to keep the focus on connection and play. By doing so, you can ensure that your sexual relationship remains a source of joy, intimacy, and fulfillment for both you and your partner.

CHAPTER TAKEAWAYS

- Sex offers emotional and psychological benefits beyond physical pleasure.
- Shifting focus from performance to connection transforms sexual experiences.
- Approaching sex as an ongoing conversation encourages fulfillment and growth.

CHAPTER 13

HOW CAN I DEAL WITH BEING REJECTED?

"**My wife never wants to have sex.**"

John came to see me because he was feeling rejected, undesirable, and as if his personal life was unraveling. His professional life was flourishing—he had the ideal job making "stupid money," owned the house of his dreams and drove the Benz he had always wanted. On the surface, everything appeared perfect. Yet, beneath this veneer of success, John's marriage was on the rocks, and he was sinking into a deep depression.

The primary source of John's distress was his wife's apparent disinterest in sex. He felt as though he was failing as a partner, unable to connect with her on the most intimate level. He didn't understand what was going wrong. Despite his efforts to initiate intimacy, he was continually met with rejection. This led to feelings of frustration, confusion, and isolation. Adding to his frustration were the constant, seemingly petty arguments about everyday things like dishes, which felt like a symptom of a much larger issue.

After listening to John, it became clear that the root of his problem wasn't just the lack of sex—it was the lack of effective communication. John had not had a meaningful conversation with his wife about their desires, intimacy, or the state of their relationship in a long time. This silence had created a chasm between them, one that couldn't be bridged by merely trying harder or setting the perfect scene for intimacy.

THE ROLE OF COMMUNICATION IN INTIMACY

John needed to learn how to communicate effectively about his needs, his feelings, and his frustrations. This was not just about expressing his desire for sex; it was about sharing his emotions—his feelings of rejection, his fear of being undesirable, and his longing for closeness. It was about having the difficult conversations that often get swept under the rug.

We started by identifying John's feelings and the underlying issues. Each week, we focused on building his communication skills and setting small, achievable targets. These included discussing his feelings with his wife at a time when they were both calm and not in the heat of an argument, as well as practicing active listening when she expressed her thoughts and emotions.

As John began to open up, something remarkable happened: his wife responded positively. She appreciated his efforts to engage in these difficult conversations, and she, too, began to share her feelings more openly. John's willingness to step out of his comfort zone and talk about these sensitive topics brought them closer together.

THE IMPORTANCE OF UNDERSTANDING YOUR PARTNER'S PERSPECTIVE

For John, sex was more than just a physical act—it was his primary way of expressing love and connecting with his wife. When she rejected his advances, it felt like she was rejecting him as a person. This feeling was compounded by his belief that sex was the only area where he could make his wife happy, and if he failed there, he was failing as a husband.

However, John needed to understand that his wife's reasons for not wanting sex were not necessarily about him. There are countless reasons why a partner might not want to engage in sex at any given time, and many of them have nothing to do with their attraction or love for their partner. These reasons can include:

- **Fatigue:** After a long day, especially if it involves taking care of children, work, or other responsibilities, the last thing someone might want is physical intimacy.
- **Stress:** High levels of stress, whether from work, family, or other sources, can drastically reduce a person's desire for sex.
- **Hormonal Changes:** Women, in particular, experience hormonal fluctuations throughout their menstrual cycle, which can affect their libido.
- **Mental Health:** Depression, anxiety, or even just a low mood can make sex seem unappealing.
- **General Disinterest:** Sometimes, it's simply a matter of not being in the mood, and it's not that deep.

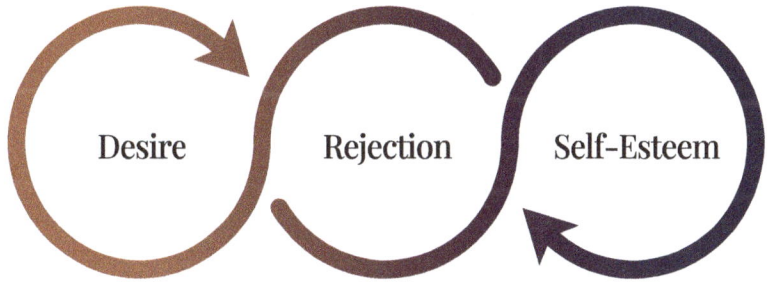

COPING WITH REJECTION

When John faced rejection, he experienced a cascade of emotions, from disappointment to embarrassment to anger. These emotions often led to behaviors that only widened the gap between him and his wife.

What's more, when you feel rejected and don't address it, it can compound the next time your partner turns you down. Learning to cope when your partner says no, and how to discuss this feeling in a constructive way, can keep you from developing resentment that eats away at your marriage or your self-esteem.

WHEN YOU WANT SEX AND YOUR PARTNER SAYS NO

Often we have a feeling or series of feelings as a result of being rejected:

What John Felt	How John Behaved	The thoughts that make it worse
Disappointment	Stop asking, withdraw emotionally, silent treatment, respond with one word answers.	"Nothing I ever do is good enough." "She's never really satisfied with me."
Embarrassed	Flip to angry responses, challenge her refusal, say something hurtful, passive aggressive comments.	"I must not be attractive." "I look foolish for even asking."
Sad	Withdraw from the relationship, seek validation elsewhere, turn to porn.	"She doesn't love me as much as I love her." "I can't make her happy." "I'm a failure in this relationship."
Lonely	Seek validation somewhere else, respond out of anger, cheat physically or emotionally.	"No one really wants me." "She doesn't care about my needs."
Hurt/upset	Angry responses, challenge her refusal, say something hurtful, passive aggressive comments.	"Why doesn't she appreciate me?" "She's doing this on purpose to hurt me."
Frustrated	Angry responses, challenge her refusal, say something hurtful, passive aggressive comments.	"She should just do this if she loves me." "My needs never come first." "This is unfair—other couples don't have this problem."

These responses created a vicious cycle. The more John reacted negatively to rejection, the more disconnected he and his wife became. This cycle of anger and disconnection drove them further apart when what John truly desired was closeness, intimacy, and companionship.

First, I'd like to assure you that if you find yourself in John's position, you are not alone. Sexual frequency changes during long-term relationships.[34] Sometimes you'll have sex several times a week and sometimes you may go months between sessions.[35] The reasons for this vary, but age, stress, and other lifestyle factors play a huge part. But just because it's normal doesn't mean you have to suffer. Let's get into how to break the cycle of rejection so you can get back to enjoying your sex life instead of worrying about it.

Breaking the Cycle: Feeling Your Emotions and Communicating

One of the most important things John learned was to feel his emotions rather than act on them immediately. Emotions, research shows, typically last no more than ninety seconds if we allow ourselves to fully experience them without judgment. However, when we suppress or ruminate on these feelings, they can linger, leading to destructive behaviors.

John began practicing a simple process: when he felt rejected, he allowed himself to sit with that emotion, acknowledging it without immediately reacting. This gave him the space to choose how he wanted to respond rather than reacting out of hurt or anger.

Once he was calm, John would approach his wife to discuss his feelings—not in the moment of rejection but at a later time when they were both more relaxed. This allowed them to have productive conversations about their relationship without the heightened emotions that often derailed their previous attempts at communication.

---

[34] Lindau, S. T., Schumm, L. P., Laumann, E. O., Levinson, W., O'Muircheartaigh, C. A., & Waite, L. J. (2007). A study of sexuality and health among older adults in the United States. *The New England Journal of Medicine, 357*(8), 762–774. https://doi.org/10.1056/NEJMoa067423.

[35] Twenge, J. M., Sherman, R. A., & Wells, B. E. (2017). Declines in sexual frequency among American adults, 1989–2014. *Archives of Sexual Behavior, 46*(8), 2389–2401. https://doi.org/10.1007/s10508-017-0953-1.

Getting Curious About Your Partner's Needs

John also learned the importance of curiosity in his relationship. Instead of assuming that his wife's rejection was about him or their relationship, he started asking questions. He wanted to understand her reasons, and in doing so, he communicated that he was interested in her well-being, not just his own desires.

For example, he would ask, "I noticed you haven't been in the mood lately—can you help me understand what's going on?" This type of open-ended question invited his wife to share her perspective, whether it was related to stress, exhaustion, or something else entirely. By showing empathy and understanding, John was able to create a space where his wife felt safe to express her feelings without fear of judgment.

Exploring Other Forms of Connection

Sex had become John's primary way of connecting with his wife, but through our sessions, he began to explore other ways to build intimacy. We discussed different activities that could foster closeness without the pressure of sex, such as:

- **Cuddling and Watching a Movie:** Physical touch without the expectation of sex can be a powerful way to connect.
- **Cuddling Naked in Bed:** This allowed them to be physically close without the pressure of intercourse.
- **Spending Time Kissing:** Focusing on kissing and other forms of non-sexual touch helped them reconnect physically in a way that felt intimate but not pressured.
- **Masturbating Next to Each Other:** This can be a way to share intimacy and pleasure without the expectation of sex.

These activities allowed John and his wife to maintain physical and emotional closeness even when sex was not on the table. By removing the pressure to perform, they were able to enjoy each other's company in a more relaxed and loving way.

The Bottom Line: Rebuilding Connection Through Understanding

What John ultimately realized was that his desire for sex was not just about physical satisfaction; it was about a deeper need for connection, intimacy, and validation. However, when he reacted to rejection with anger, frustration, or withdrawal, he was moving further away from the connection he so deeply desired.

Anger, as John learned, is not a primary emotion but a response to other underlying feelings like hurt, fear, or sadness. By addressing these underlying emotions and learning to communicate them effectively, John was able to break the cycle of disconnection.

The Solution: Moving Forward with Compassion and Curiosity

The key to rebuilding their connection was a combination of self-awareness, communication, and empathy. John's journey involved:

- **Feeling the Feeling:** Allowing himself to experience and process his emotions before reacting.
- **Communicating His Needs:** Discussing his feelings of rejection at a time when they weren't in the midst of an argument.
- **Curiosity About His Partner's Needs:** Understanding that his wife's reasons for rejecting sex were not personal and exploring other ways to connect.

As John continued to apply these lessons, he found that his relationship with his wife improved not just in the bedroom, but in every aspect of their marriage. They were able to communicate more openly, understand each other's needs more fully, and rebuild the intimacy that had been lost.

John's story is a powerful example of how effective communication, empathy, and curiosity can transform a relationship. By learning to express his needs, understand his partner's perspective, and explore new ways of connecting, John was able to rebuild the intimacy that had been lost in his marriage.

For anyone facing similar challenges, the key is to remember that intimacy is about more than just sex—it's about understanding, connection, and love. With the right tools and mindset, you can create a relationship that is not only fulfilling but deeply connected on all levels.

CHAPTER TAKEAWAYS

- Handling rejection with resilience preserves self-worth and relationship harmony.
- Sexual desire fluctuates for various reasons, often unrelated to a partner.
- Confidence and communication help maintain connection through challenges.

PART 3

SEX CHALLENGES

CHAPTER 14

SHOULD I BE USING SEX TOYS AND OTHER ENHANCERS?

Patrick came into therapy seeking help for erectile dysfunction (ED), a challenge he had struggled with for years. While he had been using Viagra with some success, the benefits were starting to wane. He was now searching for a psychological treatment option, hoping to focus, relax, and stay in the moment during intimate experiences. Patrick wanted a safe, mindful space where he could embrace pleasure, and I recommended he try a penis ring (cock ring).

Patrick, like many men, had a lot of questions when I suggested a pleasure enhancer. It's common for people to have reservations or curiosities when it comes to sex toys and aids, especially when they're introduced to something new. Many men I've worked with find that sex toys increase their enjoyment of sexual experiences, especially if their partner is having a good time too.[36] In this chapter, I will outline the most common sex toys and enhancers I recommend and answer frequently asked questions about their use. For more detailed information, including images, visit www.misterhealth.com

---

[36] Séguin, L., Watson, E., Milhausen, R., & Murray, S. (2016). The impact of a couple's vibrator on men's perceptions of their own and their partner's sexual pleasure and satisfaction. *Men and Masculinities, 19*, 370–383. https://doi.org/10.1177/1097184X15595082.

PENIS RING (COCK RING)

A penis ring is a popular device designed to help individuals who struggle with maintaining an erection. It works by placing the ring at the base of the penis, where it applies pressure to slow down blood circulation. This pressure keeps the blood in the penis, allowing the user to maintain a firmer erection for a longer period.

How to Use a Penis Ring

- Apply lubricant to the penis and the ring. This makes it easier to put on and take off.
- Gently slide the ring over the head of the penis and move it down to the base.
- Be careful not to snag the ring on pubic hair or cause any discomfort.
- After use, clean the ring with warm, soapy water and let it air dry before storing.

Tips for Choosing a Penis Ring

- Material: Consider any allergies or sensitivities, such as a latex allergy. Silicone rings are a good choice for beginners due to their flexibility.
- Fit: The ring should be snug but not painful. If you're unsure of your size, start with an adjustable ring.
- Pleasure Features: Some rings vibrate for additional stimulation, which can enhance pleasure for both partners.

DESENSITIZING SPRAY OR LOTION

Desensitizing sprays and lotions are used to delay ejaculation by slightly numbing the skin of the penis. While they can be effective, it's important to start with a small amount to avoid excessive numbness. Always test for skin irritation before extensive use.

LUBE: A MUST-HAVE FOR EVERYONE

I thought about not including lube in the enhancer chapter because, to be frank, we should all use it all the time. Lube is an essential part of a pleasurable sexual experience. It reduces friction, enhances sensations, and ensures comfort during penetration or toy use.

Types of Lubes

- Water-Based: Great for toys and condoms. It's easy to clean but may need to be reapplied during use.
- Silicone-Based: Long-lasting and great for water play but may not be compatible with silicone toys.
- Oil-Based: Not recommended for use with latex condoms but can be great for external play or massage.

DILDOS, VIBRATORS, AND PROSTATE MASSAGERS

When exploring pleasure toys, always start slow. Dildos and vibrators are great for both external and internal stimulation. For those interested in prostate play, starting with a small prostate massager can offer new and intense sensations.

Go slow, use plenty of lube, and pay attention to your body's response.

PENIS PUMP

Penis pumps are designed to help with ED by drawing blood into the penis, creating an erection. However, they don't provide a guaranteed solution and should be used with realistic expectations.

BUTT PLUGS

Exploring anal play can open up new avenues for pleasure. Remember, enjoying anal play doesn't define your sexual orientation—many straight men enjoy it. Use a well-lubricated, appropriately sized butt plug for a comfortable experience.

BONDAGE GEAR

For those looking to explore BDSM, start with beginner-friendly bondage gear like soft restraints or blindfolds. Always prioritize safety and consent and avoid using gear like handcuffs if you're not sure how to unlock them quickly.

SEX POSITIONERS

Sex positioners, like swings, wedges, or pillows, are designed to make different sexual positions more comfortable and accessible. Some of these items even have slots for toys, enhancing your experience if a partner isn't available.

Enhancing sexual pleasure is about exploration, communication, and using the right tools for you and your partner. If you've been hesitant about using pleasure enhancers, start by asking questions, experimenting with different options, and most importantly, staying present in the moment.

HESITATION ABOUT ENHANCERS

It's common for many men to feel hesitant or unsure about trying pleasure enhancers, like sex toys or aids, even though these tools can enhance sexual satisfaction. Cultural conditioning often leads men to associate their sexual prowess with their natural ability to perform, so the idea of using enhancers can bring about feelings of inadequacy or discomfort. However, it's important to understand that using pleasure enhancers is a normal and healthy part of sexual exploration, and they can add a new dimension to intimacy.

WHY SOME MEN RESIST USING TOYS OR ENHANCERS

1. **Fear of Inadequacy:** Men may worry that using toys will make them seem less capable or that their partner might rely on toys instead of them.
2. **Cultural Conditioning:** Society often portrays masculinity in a way that equates sexual success with performance. Men might feel they should be able to "perform" naturally without assistance.

3. **Lack of Knowledge:** Many men have never been exposed to these tools and are unsure how to use them or how they might enhance their experience.
4. **Feeling Uncomfortable or Embarrassed:** The thought of bringing toys into the bedroom can feel awkward or unfamiliar, especially if a man is unsure of his partner's reaction.

It's important to remind yourself that sex toys and aids are not replacements for you or your abilities, but rather tools that can enhance the sexual experience for both you and your partner. Toys can add variety, help with performance issues like ED, or simply bring a fun new element to your sex life.

HOW TO REFRAME THE IDEA OF USING ENHANCERS

- **Enhancers Are Tools, Not Replacements:** It's key to understand that toys don't replace you—they're meant to complement your experience. Just like using lube can make things more enjoyable, toys are there to enhance pleasure, not diminish your role in your partner's experience.
- **Exploration is Empowering:** Sexuality is fluid and ever-changing. Allowing yourself to explore different aspects of pleasure—whether it's with toys, new positions, or other tools—can lead to more fulfilling sexual experiences.
- **Normalize the Conversation:** Understand that using enhancers is a regular part of many people's sexual journeys. Embracing these tools doesn't mean there's something wrong with you, but rather that you're open to growth and exploration.

NAVIGATING CONVERSATIONS ABOUT ENHANCERS WITH YOUR PARTNER

Introducing the idea of using pleasure enhancers in your relationship can feel daunting, but open communication is the key to a healthy and fulfilling sex life. Here are some strategies for approaching the conversation:

1. **Start by Normalizing the Idea:** Bring up the idea of using toys or aids casually. You can reference articles, books, or even TV shows that discuss the topic, helping to normalize it before diving into your own desires or hesitations.[37]
    - Example: "I was reading about how couples use different toys to make sex even more enjoyable. What do you think about trying something new?"
2. **Frame It as a Mutual Exploration:** Instead of making it about your own needs or desires, frame it as something you can both explore together.
    - Example: "I've been thinking about how we could spice things up and add some fun to our time together. I'd love to explore some toys or enhancers with you to see what we both like."
3. **Acknowledge Any Discomfort:** If you're feeling hesitant or unsure, it's okay to express that vulnerability. Let your partner know that this is something new for you, and you're navigating it together.
    - Example: "I've never really used any toys before, and I'm a little unsure about it, but I think it could be a fun way to connect and explore more of what we both enjoy."

---

[37] Hald, G. M., Pavan, S., & Øverup, C. S. (2024). Do sex toys make me satisfied? The use of sex toys in Denmark, Norway, Sweden, Finland, France, and the UK. *The Journal of Sex Research*, 1–15. https://doi.org/10.1080/00224499.2024.2304575.

4. **Focus on the Benefits:** Emphasize how pleasure enhancers can create a more pleasurable experience for both of you. Talk about how these tools can make intimacy more exciting and enjoyable.
   - Example: "I read that using toys can really intensify sensations for both of us. I think it could be a great way for us to relax and enjoy each other even more."
5. **Be Open to Feedback:** Your partner may have their own feelings about using toys, whether it's excitement, hesitation, or curiosity. Create space for an honest conversation about their thoughts and comfort levels.
   - Example: "I want to know how you feel about this idea. I'm totally open to hearing your thoughts and making sure we both feel good about trying something new."
6. **Suggest Starting Slow:** If there's hesitation, suggest starting with something simple and small. This could be a basic vibrator, a cock ring, or some other introductory toy that's easy to use.
   - Example: "Maybe we could start with something simple, like a cock ring or a small vibrator, and see how we feel. We don't have to dive into anything too intense right away."
7. **Encourage Open Communication During Use:** Once you start using toys, encourage ongoing communication during the experience. Ask your partner how they're feeling and share your own feelings as well.
   - Example: "How does that feel? Should we try something different, or do you like this so far?"

Types of Sex Toys and Enhancers

Type of Toy	What It's Used For	Features to Look For
Penis Ring (Cock Ring)	Helps maintain erection by restricting blood flow	Adjustable size, body-safe material (e.g., silicone), optional vibration for added pleasure
Desensitizing Spray or Lotion	Delays ejaculation by numbing sensation	Mild formula, hypoallergenic, test for irritation first
Lubricant (Lube)	Reduces friction, increases comfort and sensation	Water-based for toy compatibility, silicone-based for longer-lasting use, avoid allergens
Dildo	Internal or external stimulation	Size and shape preferences, body-safe material, suction base if desired
Vibrator	Stimulates erogenous zones (clitoris, penis, nipples, etc.)	Multiple speeds/settings, rechargeable, quiet motor, waterproof if desired
Prostate Massager	Stimulates prostate for deeper pleasure and potential orgasm	Curved shape, smaller size for beginners, flared base for safety
Penis Pump	Helps achieve erection by increasing blood flow	Gauge for pressure control, comfortable seal, safety release valve
Butt Plug	Anal stimulation and prostate play	Flared base for safety, body-safe material, beginner-friendly sizing
Bondage Gear	Enhances power play or sensation play	Soft and adjustable restraints, beginner kits, safe-release options
Sex Positioners	Helps achieve or sustain different positions comfortably	Non-slip surface, supportive shape (wedges, pillows), compatibility with toys

> **CHAPTER TAKEAWAYS**
>
> - Experimenting with different pleasure techniques keeps intimacy exciting.
> - Trying new approaches fosters curiosity and shared enjoyment.
> - Novelty enhances, but deepening connection remains the key to satisfaction.

CHAPTER 15

HOW CAN I FIX ERECTILE PROBLEMS?

Sexual satisfaction is an important area of life. Unfortunately, there are a range of issues that can affect a man's ability to experience that satisfaction. Common areas of concern when it comes to male sexual function include:

- **Erectile Dysfunction (ED):** The inability to achieve or maintain an erection firm enough for sexual intercourse.
- **Premature Ejaculation (PE):** Ejaculation that occurs sooner than desired.
- **Delayed Ejaculation (DE):** Difficulty or inability to ejaculate despite prolonged sexual activity.

These conditions can affect men of all ages, but they become increasingly prevalent with age. Studies estimate that around 30% of men experience some form of sexual function concerns during their lives.[38] Here are a couple of real life examples:

BILL'S STORY

Bill sought treatment because he was struggling with premature ejaculation. Despite consulting both his primary care physician and a urologist,

---

[38] Rosen, R. C. (2000). Prevalence and risk factors of sexual dysfunction in men and women. *Current Psychiatry Reports, 2*, 189–195. https://doi.org/10.1007/s11920-996-0006-2.

who assured him there was nothing medically wrong, he felt hopeless about overcoming the issue. Bill wasn't someone who typically believed in therapy and was very anxious about making the call to schedule an appointment. He initially thought the whole process was nonsense, but his desperation pushed him to give it a try. Willing to do whatever was needed, we scheduled a session.

Bill shared that he had been dealing with this issue for about fifteen years, but it only occurred during partnered sex, which made him feel extremely self-conscious. We discussed various methods, including the start-stop technique and mindfulness practices, to help him connect more deeply with his body and mind. It became clear that Bill wasn't aware of when he was about to ejaculate—it just happened, as he described.

We explored techniques like Sensate Focus to help him slow down and gain a better understanding of his body. By paying more attention to his body, particularly his penis and arousal, Bill began to notice significant improvements. He was able to last longer during sex and, importantly, experience more pleasure.

ANOTHER TYPE OF PROBLEM

Peter came into therapy because he was experiencing delayed ejaculation. The problem had started several months after a difficult breakup with his long-term girlfriend. He reported that it often took him 45 minutes to an hour to ejaculate, and sometimes, he wouldn't ejaculate at all, giving up in frustration. Peter was still deeply upset about the breakup and was bottling up a lot of emotions. He felt like he had failed in many ways, and the idea of finding another partner seemed overwhelming. These thoughts would often surface during sex, making it hard for Peter to stay in the moment.

Post-breakup, Peter was second-guessing himself, lacking confidence, and struggling to see himself as lovable. While these issues were contributing to his delayed ejaculation, the underlying cause was the significant anxiety and depression he was experiencing.

We focused on processing the breakup and helping Peter get his life back on track. As he started to feel more stable in those areas, he was ready to address his delayed ejaculation. Through therapy, Peter developed new coping skills and noticed a significant improvement in his symptoms. He was surprised and relieved to find that it no longer took him 45 minutes to ejaculate; instead, he was able to do so in 15 to 20 minutes. Addressing his anxiety and regaining his confidence made all the difference.

THERE ARE SOLUTIONS

Dealing with sexual function issues can be stressful, but there are solutions. It is crucial that men understand this fact and pursue treatments when issues arise. The worst thing you can do is hide from the problem. Denial and defensiveness are not helpful. The intention of this chapter is to make sure you have the information you need to address sexual function and regain the sexual experiences you want.

PERFORMANCE ANXIETY? COULD BE

It could be performance anxiety. Several studies have found distinct links between performance anxiety and sexual function for men.[39] Even when you consider other causes such as stress/fatigue levels, communication, and sexual attitudes, performance anxiety was the only unique predictor of sexual dysfunction. For more on performance anxiety, see Chapter 17.

---

[39] Bockaj, A., Muise, M. D., Belu, C. F., Rosen, N. O., & O'Sullivan, L. F. (2024). Under pressure: Men's and women's sexual performance anxiety in the sexual interactions of adult couples. *The Journal of Sex Research*, 1–13. https://doi.org/10.1080/00224499.2024.2357587.

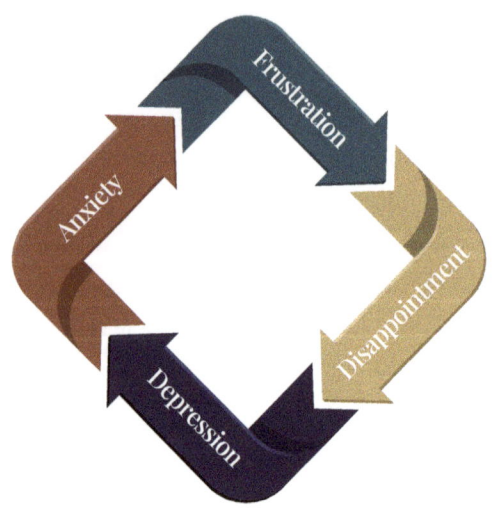

THE IMPORTANCE OF ADDRESSING SEXUAL FUNCTION ISSUES

Addressing male sexual function concerns is crucial. Avoiding the issue can have far-reaching impacts on a man's life.[40] Let's look at a few of the potential consequences:

- **Impact on Self-Esteem:** Sexual performance is often closely tied to a man's sense of self-worth. When issues like ED or PE arise, they can lead to feelings of inadequacy, shame, and anxiety. Over time, these feelings can erode self-confidence and contribute to a negative self-image.
- **Effects on Relationships:** Sexual function concerns can strain relationships, causing tension, frustration, and a sense of disconnect between partners. Without open communication and support, these challenges can lead to misunderstandings, decreased intimacy, and even the breakdown of the relationship.

---

[40] Yale Medicine. (n.d.). *Erectile dysfunction.* https://www.yalemedicine.org/news/erectile-dysfunction.

- **Overall Well-Being:** Sexual health is a vital component of overall well-being. When sexual function concerns go unaddressed, it can contribute to mental health issues such as depression and anxiety, as well as physical health problems related to stress and frustration. Addressing sexual function concerns early and comprehensively can improve sexual health and enhance your overall quality of life.

POTENTIAL MEDICAL ISSUES

While emotional issues may be the first to come to mind when we think about sexual function concerns, physical health may be an issue as well.[41] Physical health plays a significant role in sexual performance, and various medical conditions can contribute to male sexual dysfunction. For example:

- **Cardiovascular Issues:** Conditions like high blood pressure, atherosclerosis (hardening of the arteries), and heart disease can impair blood flow to the penis, leading to erectile dysfunction (ED). The health of the cardiovascular system is crucial for maintaining an erection, as proper blood flow is necessary for penile rigidity.
- **Diabetes:** Men with diabetes are at a higher risk of developing ED due to damage to blood vessels and nerves. Poorly managed blood sugar levels can lead to neuropathy, which affects the nerves responsible for arousal and erection.
- **Hormonal Imbalances:** Low levels of testosterone, the primary male sex hormone, can decrease libido and contribute to ED. Hormonal imbalances, including thyroid issues or elevated levels of prolactin, can also impact sexual function.

---

[41] Cleveland Clinic. (n.d.). *Sexual dysfunction.* https://my.clevelandclinic.org/health/diseases/9121-sexual-dysfunction *(Accessed January 28, 2025).*

CONSULTING A UROLOGIST OR DOCTOR

While recent decades indicate a shift, men are significantly less likely to seek help from sexual wellness professionals than women.[42] Given the potential medical causes of sexual function issues, it is crucial to consult a urologist or medical professional if you are experiencing symptoms like ED, premature ejaculation (PE), or delayed ejaculation (DE). A healthcare professional can:

- **Conduct a Thorough Evaluation:** Your doctor will assess your medical history, perform physical examinations, and may order tests to identify any underlying conditions contributing to your sexual dysfunction.
- **Provide Targeted Treatment:** Once a medical issue is identified, your doctor can recommend appropriate treatments. This may include medications to manage blood pressure or diabetes, hormone replacement therapy, or other interventions tailored to your specific needs.
- **Offer Guidance and Support:** A healthcare professional can also guide lifestyle changes that can improve sexual health, such as diet, exercise, and stress management. They can help you understand the connection between your overall health and sexual performance, empowering you to take proactive steps toward improvement.

THE MIND-BODY DISCONNECT

A key factor in male sexual function is the connection between the brain and the body. When there is a disconnect, even when the mind is ready for sex, the body may not respond as expected. For instance, you may

---

[42] Pearson, S. (2003). Men's use of sexual health services. *Journal of Family Planning and Reproductive Health Care, 29*(4), 190–194. https://doi.org/10.1783/147118903101198060.

feel mentally aroused and eager to engage in sexual activity. Still, your body might not cooperate, resulting in difficulties such as erectile dysfunction (ED) or delayed ejaculation (DE). This can happen for a number of reasons.

The Fight-or-Flight Response

One major contributor to this disconnect is the body's fight-or-flight response, a natural reaction to stress or anxiety. When faced with a stressful situation, the body automatically shifts into survival mode. The immediate response is to protect ourselves, seek ways of feeling safe, and eliminate functions that are not essential for survival. Sexual activity is not a priority during the fight-or-flight response.

This response is helpful in dangerous situations but is obviously detrimental during sexual experiences. When you are anxious or stressed—whether due to concerns about performance, relationship issues, or external pressures—your body may become tense and enter a state of heightened alertness. This inhibits the relaxation and physical arousal needed for satisfying sexual performance. Instead of engaging in the sexual experience, your body remains on high alert, making it difficult to achieve or maintain an erection or to experience pleasure.

Recognizing when your body is in fight-or-flight mode and learning techniques to relax and reconnect with your physical sensations can help restore harmony between your mind and body, improving your sexual experience.

Psychological and Emotional Factors

Mental health also plays a critical role in sexual function, and issues such as anxiety, depression, and trauma can significantly contribute to male sexual function issues.

- **Anxiety:** Performance anxiety, in particular, is a common issue that can lead to erectile dysfunction or premature ejaculation.

The fear of not performing well can create a self-fulfilling prophecy, where the stress itself inhibits the ability to engage in or enjoy sexual activity.
- **Depression:** Depression can dampen sexual desire and energy levels, making it difficult to become aroused or maintain an erection. It can also lead to a lack of interest in sexual activity altogether, further exacerbating the problem.
- **Trauma:** Past traumatic experiences, especially those related to sex or relationships, can deeply affect your ability to engage in healthy sexual activity. Trauma can trigger feelings like fear, shame, or discomfort during intimate moments, leading to sexual function issues.

These psychological factors often contribute to what can be described as a mental loop—a cycle of worry and overthinking that further intensifies sexual function concerns.

- **The Cycle of Worry:** When anxiety about sexual performance sets in, it can create a vicious cycle. A man might worry about whether he'll be able to maintain an erection or last long enough during sex. This worry then triggers physical symptoms of anxiety, such as increased heart rate, sweating, and muscle tension, which can disrupt the natural flow of sexual arousal. The more one worries about performance, the more likely it is that the dysfunction will occur, which only adds to the anxiety in future sexual encounters.
- **The Logical Brain vs. Sexual Self:** Sexual experiences are deeply rooted in emotions and physical sensations. However, when anxiety takes over, the logical brain tries to take control by focusing on outcomes and logistics—how long you last, whether you'll be able to maintain an erection, or if your partner is satisfied. This shift from emotional engagement to logistical thinking pulls you out of the moment, making it harder

to connect with your sexual self. As a result, the experience becomes mechanical rather than intimate, leading to further disconnection and frustration.

EMOTIONAL CONSEQUENCES

When a man experiences ongoing sexual dysfunction, it can lead to intense feelings of frustration and embarrassment. The repeated failure to meet sexual expectations—whether self-imposed or perceived from a partner—can result in a negative self-perception. Men may start to view themselves as "broken" or "inadequate," which can erode confidence in the bedroom and other areas of life.

This frustration is often compounded by embarrassment, particularly if the sexual function issues occur during intimate moments with a partner. The fear of disappointing a partner or being judged can lead to a reluctance to engage in sexual activity, creating a cycle of avoidance that further distances the individual from healthy sexual expression.

These feelings of frustration and embarrassment can, over time, spiral into deeper emotional issues. The persistent struggle with sexual dysfunction may lead to a descent into a "dark place," where negative emotions become overwhelming.

- **Depression:** Depression can lead to sexual function issues, but sexual function issues can also lead to depression. The constant stress and disappointment associated with sexual concerns may lead to feelings of hopelessness about their sexual abilities. This can affect their overall mental health.
- **Loss of Sexual Desire:** As the emotional toll of sexual function issues grows, men may experience a loss of sexual desire altogether. The fear of failure and the pain of repeated disappointments can make the idea of sex seem more like a source of anxiety than pleasure. This withdrawal from sexual activity

can further isolate men from their partners, leading to feelings of loneliness and despair.

BREAKING THE CYCLE

Things can change. You do not have to stay in the cycle of frustration and disappointment. Anxiety and depression do not need to define your sex life. You can break the cycle and recapture the sexual activity you want.

Understanding the Role of Presence and Sensation

A key to overcoming male sexual function concerns lies in reconnecting with your body and emotions. Presence—being fully engaged in the moment—allows you to tune into your physical sensations and emotional responses during sexual activity. This focus on the here and now helps you break free from the anxiety and overthinking that often accompany sexual function issues. Instead of getting lost in worries about performance, you become more attuned to what your body is actually experiencing. That may mean focusing on the way your penis feels, but let's go beyond that, especially if you find yourself worrying about your erection. You begin to notice the texture of your partner's skin, the rhythm of your breath, and the warmth of touch. This mindful approach can help shift your focus from outcome to experience and reduce the pressure.

Moving Beyond the Logical Brain

Sexual experiences are far more than just a series of mechanical processes. While the logical brain might try to control the situation by focusing on steps and outcomes, this approach is counterproductive. Sexuality is deeply rooted in emotional and sensory experiences, which require a different kind of engagement. It involves letting go of control and allowing yourself to be vulnerable and emotionally connected.

When you rely solely on your logical brain, you may miss out on the richness of the experience, turning what should be an intimate and pleasurable moment into a task to be completed. Instead, by moving beyond this logistical mindset and embracing the full range of sensations, you can cultivate a more fulfilling and responsive sexual experience.

PRACTICAL STRATEGIES

Fortunately, there are several techniques and tools available to help manage and overcome sexual function concerns.

Creating a Supportive Environment

Setting up an environment that encourages relaxation and connection is another crucial step in breaking the cycle of sexual dysfunction. Here are some tips:

- **Eliminate Distractions:** Create a space that is free from distractions like phones, loud noises, or interruptions. This allows you to focus solely on the experience at hand.
- **Set the Mood:** Consider using dim lighting, soft music, or candles to create a calming atmosphere. These elements can help reduce anxiety and make the environment more conducive to intimacy.
- **Communicate Openly with Your Partner:** Discussing your feelings and concerns with your partner can alleviate some of the pressure you may feel. Open communication fosters trust and connection, making it easier to relax and be present.

- **Focus on Connection, Not Performance:** Shift your focus from trying to perform perfectly to simply enjoying the connection with your partner. This mindset can help reduce performance anxiety and make the experience more enjoyable.

Mindfulness

Mindfulness is a powerful tool for reconnecting with your body during sexual experiences. By focusing on the present moment and fully immersing yourself in the physical sensations you are experiencing, you can reduce anxiety and enhance sexual pleasure. Try these mindful practices:

- **Deep Breathing:** Practice slow, deep breaths to calm your nervous system and bring your focus back to your body. This helps to reduce the fight-or-flight response that can inhibit sexual performance.
- **Progressive Muscle Relaxation:** Gradually tense and relax different muscle groups in your body to release physical tension and increase your awareness of how your body feels in the moment.
- **Guided Visualization:** Picture a peaceful, relaxing scene in your mind. This can help shift your focus away from performance anxiety and toward the positive sensations in your body.

Cognitive Behavioral Techniques (CBT)

Cognitive behavioral techniques (CBT) offer practical ways to challenge and change the negative thought patterns that contribute to sexual dysfunction. CBT involves recognizing unhelpful thoughts—such as "I always fail" or "My partner is going to be disappointed"—and replacing them with more balanced, realistic perspectives. Men who use CBT as part of their treatment plan for ED see significant improvement that lasts long after treatment stops.[43]

- **Identify Negative Thoughts:** Pay attention to the thoughts that arise during sexual activity. Are you catastrophizing, assuming the worst, or engaging in black-and-white thinking?
- **Challenge These Thoughts:** Once you've identified a negative thought, question its validity. Ask yourself if there is evidence to support this belief or if it's simply a product of anxiety.
- **Replace With Positive Affirmations:** Replace negative thoughts with positive affirmations that reinforce your confidence and ability to enjoy the experience. For example, instead of thinking, "I'm going to mess up," you might remind yourself, "I'm here to enjoy this moment with my partner, and that's what matters."

Open Communication with Partners

Open and honest communication with your partner is essential for addressing sexual dysfunction and fostering a deeper connection. Discussing your fears, expectations, and experiences can create a more supportive and understanding environment.

- **Share Your Feelings:** Let your partner know what you're experiencing, whether it's anxiety, frustration, or a lack of confidence. This openness can help demystify the issue and reduce the pressure you feel.
- **Set Mutual Expectations:** Discuss what both of you expect from your sexual relationship. This can help alleviate

---

[43] Khan, S., Amjad, A., & Rowland, D. (2019). Potential for long-term benefit of cognitive behavioral therapy as an adjunct treatment for men with erectile dysfunction. *Journal of Sexual Medicine, 16*(2), 300–306. https://doi.org/10.1016/j.jsxm.2018.12.014.

misunderstandings and ensure both partners feel heard and valued.
- **Explore Together:** Use your sexual experiences as an opportunity to explore each other's desires and boundaries. This can help strengthen your bond and make the experience more enjoyable for both of you.

Sensory Awareness Exercise

One powerful exercise to help address male sexual function concerns involves developing a deeper awareness of your body's responses to sexual stimuli. This exercise is designed to help you reconnect with your physical sensations and emotions.

Observing Your Body's Reactions to Sexual Stimuli

1. **Set the Stage**
    - Find a quiet, comfortable place where you can lie down naked. A bed is ideal, but any space where you can relax without distractions will work.
    - Take a few deep breaths to center yourself and let go of any tension.
2. **Focus on Erotic Thoughts**
    - Without using pornography or external stimuli, bring an erotic thought or fantasy to mind. This could be a memory, a scenario, or an idea you find arousing.
    - Allow yourself to fully engage with this thought, but keep your focus on what's happening within your body.
3. **Tune Into Your Body**
    - **Notice the First Sensations**
      As you begin to feel aroused, observe the first physical sensations that arise. What do you notice first? Is it a change in your breathing? A flutter in your stomach?

- **Track the Changes**
  Continue to pay attention as these sensations evolve. How does your body change as your arousal builds? Does your heart rate increase? Do certain areas of your body start to tingle or feel warm?
4. **Explore Specific Areas**
   - **Breath and Stomach**
     Notice how your breathing patterns shift as you become more aroused. Does your stomach tighten or relax?
   - **Touch and Sensitivity**
     Which parts of your body seem to crave touch? Do you feel a desire to move or change positions as your arousal deepens?
   - **Erection Sensations**
     Pay attention to any changes in your penis without looking at it. Do you develop an erection? If so, how does it feel? If it's a partial erection, what are the sensations like? Focus on how your body experiences this without the need for visual confirmation.
5. **Stay Present**
   - The key to this exercise is to remain fully present with your body's sensations. Avoid drifting into logistics or judgments about your performance. Instead, allow yourself to experience what's happening moment by moment.

This exercise encourages you to reconnect with your body's natural responses, free from the pressure of performance or the distractions of external stimuli like pornography. Over time, this practice can help you develop a more relaxed and connected approach to sexual experiences, improving both your physical responses and your emotional well-being.[44]

---

[44] Baxter, R. (n.d.). What is Sensate Focus and how does it work? *SMSNA*. https://www.smsna.org/patients/did-you-know/what-is-sensate-focus-and-how-does-it-work.

The Start-Stop Method

The Start-Stop Method developed by Masters and Johnson, often referred to as "edging," is a technique that can be particularly helpful for men dealing with premature ejaculation, but it's also beneficial for other sexual challenges.[45]

- **How It Works:** The idea behind the Start-Stop Method is to become more attuned to your body's signals during sexual activity. As you approach the point of ejaculation, you intentionally stop the stimulation before reaching the "point of no return"—the moment when ejaculation becomes inevitable.
- **Why It Helps:** By practicing this technique, you learn to recognize the subtle sensations and signs that your body is nearing climax. This increased awareness allows you to gain more control over your sexual response, helping you delay ejaculation and extend sexual activity. Over time, this practice can significantly reduce the anxiety associated with sexual performance and give you greater confidence in managing your sexual experiences.

The Use of Sex Toys

Sex toys can also play a valuable role in addressing male sexual dysfunction, particularly erectile dysfunction. Here are a few examples:

- **Cock Rings:** Cock rings are designed to help maintain an erection by restricting blood flow out of the penis. While they are often used by men who experience difficulty maintaining an erection due to blood flow issues, they can also enhance the

---

[45] Doğan, K., & Keçe, C. (2023). Comparison of the results of stop-start technique with stop-start technique and sphincter control training applied in premature ejaculation treatment. *PLOS ONE, 18*(8), e0283091. https://doi.org/10.1371/journal.pone.0283091.

firmness of an erection even when blood flow isn't the primary concern. Cock rings are easy to use and can be a practical solution for men looking to improve their sexual performance.
- **Desensitizing Sprays or Lotions:** These products can be used by men who experience premature ejaculation. Desensitizing sprays or lotions reduce the sensitivity of the penis, allowing for longer-lasting sexual activity. Applying a small amount of these products before sexual activity can increase your control over ejaculation.

You can visit chapter 14 on sexual enhancers for more information.

Combining Techniques for Better Results

You can mix and match these practical strategies for even better results. While the Start-Stop Method and the use of sex toys are effective on their own, combining these methods can provide even greater benefits. Mindfulness, sensory awareness, and cognitive behavioral techniques can all be part of the same strategy. Explore, experiment, and most of all, enjoy.

THINGS TO KNOW

Sexual function concerns are not unusual. It is a common issue, but there are plenty of solutions.

- See a healthcare professional to assess any potential physical issues such as high blood pressure or diabetes.
- Explore any emotional, psychological, or relationship issues that may be affecting sexual function.
- Break the cycle of worry and overthinking through practical strategies and exercises.

With the proper techniques, practices, and support, you can deal with sexual function issues and keep your sexual life thriving.

> **CHAPTER TAKEAWAYS**
>
> - Understanding common performance issues helps address them effectively.
> - Practical techniques support better erectile function and ejaculatory control.
> - Viewing sexual challenges as normal reduces stress and improves outcomes.

CHAPTER 16

WHY DO I GET SO NERVOUS ABOUT SEX AND HOW CAN I STOP?

The silent struggle for many men is fear and sexual insecurity. Fears about their performance, their bodies, and their ability to satisfy a partner. These insecurities can stem from societal pressures, unrealistic standards, and personal experiences that shape how men view themselves sexually.

One of the mantras I hear most in therapy sessions with men is: "I can't fuck this up." This statement reveals a deep-rooted anxiety about failing sexually and the potential consequences that follow. It speaks to a pervasive fear of not meeting expectations—both self-imposed and those perceived from others—and the possibility of facing rejection or judgment as a result.

In this chapter, I want to explore these insecurities with empathy and openness. The goal is to move beyond the shame and pressure and set the stage for acceptance and understanding. I want to empower you to embrace vulnerabilities, recognize the reality of your experiences, and find healthier ways to view yourself and your sexual relationships. This journey is not about perfection but about growth, self-compassion, and the pursuit of genuine connections.

MARK'S STORY

Mark came to see me because he was having a lot of performance anxiety and just couldn't get out of his head. When he would have sex with his partner, he would often replay the message "I can't mess this up."

Without fail, this would kill his erection and put him into full panic mode. He didn't understand why this was happening because he was trying so hard to not lose his erection.

His partner would often get irritated and say, "Mark, you aren't present. What are you thinking about? Why can't you just be here with me?" The narratives his partner built up was that Mark was thinking about more important things or potentially other people.

Mark struggled bringing himself back to the present. The solution was for him to practice this outside and inside the sexual experience. Mark started developing the skill to identify his thoughts quicker so he could bring himself back to the present moment. He began focusing on thoughts like, "Mark, look how beautiful your partner is," "Focus on how good this feels," and "Focus on being playful and having fun."

After a lot of practice, Mark was getting better at these new thought patterns and made significant progress. He and his partner were much happier as a result.

COMMON MALE SEXUAL INSECURITIES

Mark isn't the only one dealing with these problems. It is an all too common male issue. The sexual insecurities that men often experience can deeply impact their self-esteem and relationships. Here are some of the most common insecurities men face:

Penis Size

One of the most pervasive insecurities among men is penis size. The cultural obsession with size stems from a belief that a larger penis equates to better sexual performance and greater masculinity. This idea is often reinforced by media, pornography, and societal standards that equate a man's worth with his physical attributes.

In a study from National Institute for Health Research, a group of men all fell in the average range for penis size of 7 to 13 centimeters;

however, most participants started to think their penis was too small around sixteen years of age.[46] Their worry about the size of their penis increased the prevalence of erectile dysfunction, and decreased both orgasmic function and intercourse satisfaction for the men. Since all of these men fell in the typical range, researchers found that the anxiety about size was the problem, not the actual size. This fixation on size overlooks reality. Sexual satisfaction involves far more than anatomy.

Technique

The pressure to perform sexually can be overwhelming. Men often worry about their ability to satisfy their partner, fearing they lack the right "technique" or skills. This anxiety can be compounded by the unrealistic portrayals of sex in media, which often present an idealized version of intimacy that's more about showmanship than genuine connection.

Remember, what you see on the screen is a choreographed scene with professional actors. Unwarranted comparisons can lead to fear of being unable to please a partner. It can lead to a cycle of stress and self-doubt, where men feel they must constantly prove their sexual prowess.

Performance Anxiety

Closely related to concerns about technique, performance anxiety is a widespread issue that involves fear of "messing up" during sex. This anxiety can stem from a single negative experience or a general fear of inadequacy. Men may worry about issues like erectile dysfunction, premature ejaculation, or simply not living up to expectations. The fear of these potential mishaps can create a high-pressure environment where the focus shifts from mutual pleasure to avoiding mistakes. For many,

---

[46] Veale, D., Miles, S., Read, J., Troglia, A., Wylie, K., & Muir, G. (2015). Sexual functioning and behavior of men with body dysmorphic disorder concerning penis size compared with men anxious about penis size and with controls: A cohort study. *Sexual Medicine, 3*(3), 147–155. https://doi.org/10.1002/sm2.63.

the idea of not meeting their partner's expectations is tied to deeper fears of rejection and the loss of emotional connection.

Body Image Issues

Beyond sexual performance, many men experience insecurities related to their overall body image. Concerns about muscle size, body hair, weight, and balding can contribute to feelings of inadequacy and self-consciousness. Just as women are bombarded with images of idealized beauty, men also face societal pressures to conform to a particular physical ideal. These insecurities can affect how men view themselves sexually and emotionally, leading to a lack of confidence and a reluctance to be vulnerable with their partners.

Understanding these common insecurities is the first step toward addressing them. It's important to recognize that these fears are rooted in societal pressures and unrealistic expectations rather than actual deficiencies. Shining a light on these insecurities can help you break free from shame and anxiety. You can develop a new perspective and move toward a healthier, more accepting view of yourself.

THE REAL FEAR BEHIND THE INSECURITIES

While male sexual insecurities often manifest as concerns about physical attributes or sexual performance, they are usually rooted in deeper emotion. Let's look at some of the potential issues.

Fear of Rejection and Loss

The fear of rejection is not just about a single moment of embarrassment but the potential for losing a partner. This fear is present even in casual sexual encounters, where the stakes might seem lower. The idea that a partner could leave, withdraw affection, or mock you after a perceived sexual failure creates a powerful sense of anxiety.

For men, especially those who equate their worth with their ability to satisfy a partner, the prospect of losing someone due to sexual inadequacy can be devastating. The root of this fear can stem from a desire for acceptance and a need to feel valued and wanted in intimate relationships.

The truth is, rejection is a universal experience and an inevitable part of life. While inherently painful, it is also integral to personal growth and self-discovery. Everyone, at some point, faces rejection in various forms—be it romantic, professional, or social. Not every relationship is meant to continue.

It's important to recognize that rejection does not define your worth or ability to connect with others. The fear of rejection is natural, but learning to navigate and accept it is crucial for developing emotional resilience.

Rejection is not a reflection of your value. It is a common part of the human experience. To put it bluntly, it happens. This understanding can lessen the power these insecurities hold over you.

The Social Pressure of Performance

Much of the anxiety surrounding male sexual insecurities is amplified by social pressures and cultural norms. Men are often expected to be strong, confident, and sexually adept. There is an unspoken expectation that we should always know what to do in the bedroom and perform without fail.

No man wants to be the subject of ridicule or seen as less than ideal. This pressure is particularly intense in a culture that often equates masculinity with sexual prowess. As a result, you may feel that you must constantly prove yourself to avoid being perceived as less than a "real man."

TOO OFTEN, MEN SUFFER IN SILENCE

A study from *BMC Health Services Research* found that men often internalize the traditionally masculine traits of assertiveness and self-assurance, which is in opposition to asking for help with sexual issues.[47] The vulnerability required to tackle sexual health concerns with a doctor or therapist is often too difficult for men and leads them to take sexual risks and avoid seeking healthcare. The truth is tackling sexual health issues with your partner or your healthcare providers is brave and strong, even if it's hard. My hope is that by using this book you can develop the tools for identifying what is wrong and find the strength to communicate about it.

CHALLENGING THE NEGATIVE SELF-TALK

When the inner dialogue is, "I can't fuck this up," it represents a deep-seated anxiety about sexual performance. This mindset reflects a belief that any mistake in the bedroom could lead to severe consequences, such as feeling weak, being perceived as less masculine, or losing a partner. To challenge this belief, let's explore what happens if things don't go as planned.

What Happens If You Do?

Be honest about what you fear if something goes wrong. Is it a catastrophic failure? Is it simply a fear of embarrassment, or does it touch on broader concerns about your masculinity and worth? Are you concerned about your partner's disappointment, or do you fear the end of

---

[47] Persson, T., Löve, J., Tengelin, E., & Hensing, G. (2023). Healthcare professionals' discourses on men and masculinities in sexual healthcare: A focus group study. *BMC Health Services Research, 23*(1), 535. https://doi.org/10.1186/s12913-023-09508-2.

the relationship? Facing up to your fears is the first step to dealing with them. Knowing the actual fear is much better than a vague, dark fear ruminating in your mind.

Following the Thought to Its Root

The fear of failing in bed is often less about the act itself and more about what it represents: a fear of losing connection and being judged. For many men, sexual performance is linked to their sense of identity and self-worth. They might worry that if they don't perform well, their partner will stop seeing them as desirable or worthy of love.

This fear is really about wanting acceptance and validation, needing to feel valued and respected in a relationship. The anxiety about "messing up" is more about the fear of rejection and losing intimacy than about the actual sexual act.

Understanding that these fears come from a deeper place can help you let go of unrealistic expectations. It's important to realize that making a mistake in bed doesn't define your worth or masculinity. Everyone has moments of vulnerability, and these don't lessen your value.

By focusing on the real source of these fears, you can approach your sexual experiences with more self-compassion and less worry about performance. Ultimately, it's about authenticity, not perfection.

ACCEPTING INSECURITIES AND FOCUSING ON REALITY

Acknowledging sexual insecurities is the beginning, but there is more to do. The next step is a shift in mindset that embraces both acceptance and self-improvement. Among the most challenging yet essential steps is learning to lean into discomfort, distinguishing between what can and cannot be changed, and avoiding the pitfalls of toxic positivity.

Leaning into Discomfort

Many men try to avoid situations where they might feel inadequate or exposed, but this avoidance only reinforces fear and anxiety. Instead, learning to lean into discomfort means embracing vulnerability and recognizing that it's okay to be imperfect. The truth is that everyone faces rejection at some point, and fearing it only gives it more power.

It's about understanding that your worth isn't defined by any single experience or moment of perceived failure.

Acceptance vs. Change

Another crucial element of overcoming insecurities is distinguishing between what can be changed and what cannot. Concerns about penis size, for example, are largely unfounded and rooted in unrealistic societal standards. Accepting that this is something that cannot be altered is an important step toward self-acceptance. On the other hand, if insecurities are related to something changeable, like muscle size or fitness levels, you can work towards the improvements that make you happy in a healthy, balanced way.

The key is to set realistic expectations and understand that personal growth should be motivated by self-love and the desire for well-being, not external validation. Accepting certain aspects of yourself while choosing to improve others creates a healthier self-perception and reduces the pressure to conform to unrealistic ideals.

Avoiding Toxic Positivity

While positivity can be beneficial, it becomes toxic when it denies reality or forces you to suppress genuine feelings. Telling someone to "just be positive" or "ignore the haters" often dismisses their legitimate concerns and experiences. Instead of relying on empty slogans, embrace reality and face insecurities head-on.

This means acknowledging what bothers you without judgment and then deciding how to approach it with wisdom, compassion, and clarity. Real growth comes from recognizing your strengths and insecurities and choosing to work on them authentically, not from pretending they don't exist or insisting they shouldn't matter. Focus on what is real and embrace a more balanced perspective. This will allow you to cultivate genuine self-acceptance and develop a healthier approach to those insecurities.

FINDING VALIDATION BEYOND PHYSICAL TRAITS

Finding validation solely through physical attributes can be both fleeting and limiting. To cultivate a healthier sense of self, let's explore alternative ways to find genuine validation.

Validation plays a critical role in shaping self-esteem and emotional resilience. It influences how we see ourselves and how we interact with the world. However, there are two primary sources of validation: internal and external, and understanding the distinction between them can empower us to cultivate a more balanced and fulfilling sense of self.

Internal Validation: Building Confidence from Within

Internal validation comes from recognizing and affirming your own worth, abilities, and emotions without relying on external approval. It involves:

- Self-acceptance: Understanding and embracing who you are, flaws and all.
- Personal values: Making choices based on what aligns with your beliefs and goals.

- Resilience: Bouncing back from challenges without needing constant reassurance from others.
- Self-compassion: Being kind to yourself and acknowledging your efforts and progress.

When you cultivate internal validation, you create a strong foundation of self-worth that isn't easily shaken by external opinions or societal pressures. This leads to greater emotional stability, independence, and overall mental well-being.

External Validation: Seeking Approval from Others

External validation, on the other hand, is the affirmation and recognition we receive from others—whether it's praise from friends, social media likes, or professional achievements. While external validation can boost confidence and provide motivation, over-reliance on it can be problematic.

Some key aspects of external validation include:

- Social feedback: Compliments and encouragement from peers, family, or colleagues.
- Achievement recognition: Awards, promotions, or public acknowledgment of accomplishments.
- Approval seeking: Modifying behaviors or decisions to gain acceptance from others.

While external validation is a natural and sometimes necessary part of life, relying solely on it can create feelings of insecurity, self-doubt, and dependence on others for happiness. It can also make individuals vulnerable to societal pressures and unrealistic standards.

Why Both Forms of Validation Matter

A healthy balance between internal and external validation is crucial. Internal validation fosters self-confidence and authenticity, while external validation helps build social connections and encourages growth. When these two forms of validation work together, they contribute to a more well-rounded and emotionally resilient individual.

Striking the Right Balance Means:

- Using external validation as a complement, not a necessity.
- Developing self-awareness and self-acceptance to fuel internal validation.
- Recognizing when external validation is driving your decisions instead of your values.

Ultimately, by prioritizing internal validation while appreciating the support and recognition of others, you can achieve a greater sense of self-worth and emotional stability.

Finding Validation in Healthier Ways

Moving past seeking validation through physical traits means recognizing that true self-worth comes from within, not from how we look or the approval of others. Embracing self-worth involves understanding that our value is not tied to our appearance but to our qualities, actions, and character. It's about fostering self-compassion, celebrating our unique strengths, and building confidence in who we are, rather than relying on external validation. By focusing on inner growth and self-acceptance, we can create a healthier and more fulfilling sense of self.

Cultural Conditioning Around Male Appearance

Moving past cultural conditioning around male appearance means challenging the stereotypes and expectations that society imposes on men. This involves recognizing that worth isn't determined by muscle size, facial hair, or any specific physical trait. Instead of striving to fit into narrow definitions of masculinity, embrace diverse expressions of male identity and appearance. Reject the limiting standards men too often imposed by society, and prioritize your own comfort, well-being, and authenticity. This is a plan that leads to a more inclusive and accepting view of what it means to be a man.

PRACTICING EMOTIONAL RESILIENCE

Building emotional resilience is essential for overcoming insecurities and developing a healthier relationship with yourself. Instead of avoiding uncomfortable emotions like fear of rejection or inadequacy, learning to sit with these feelings can enhance self-awareness and emotional strength. Here are some exercises to help you practice resilience, understand how long emotions last, and become more comfortable with vulnerability and rejection. The goal is to feel the feelings, not shove them away or ignore them.

Sitting with Discomfort

We've already discussed the importance of leaning into discomfort. Here is an exercise you can try to put this into practice. Recall a time when you felt rejected or insecure. Notice the emotional and physical responses that arise—such as tension in your chest, a knot in your stomach, or a lump in your throat. By observing these sensations without judgment or the need to change them, you can build a tolerance for discomfort.

Over time, this practice makes emotions feel less overwhelming and more manageable.

Understanding Emotional Duration

When emotions arise, they can feel all-encompassing, but they are actually temporary. By recognizing that emotions are fleeting and allowing them to pass naturally, you can learn to move through difficult feelings without being controlled by them. Mindfulness techniques, like deep breathing or grounding exercises, can help manage the intensity of emotions and let them fade more quickly. The goal is not to avoid emotions but to become more comfortable experiencing them and letting them go.

Building Emotional Strength

Developing emotional strength involves becoming more comfortable with the possibility of rejection and not letting it affect your self-worth. To build this type of strength, try putting yourself in situations where there's a chance of distress, such as trying a new activity, speaking up in a group, or starting a tough conversation. Each time you face discomfort, you strengthen your resilience and learn that you can thrive despite these experiences. Remember, rejection doesn't reflect your value as a person; it's an opportunity for growth and learning. By viewing rejection as a natural part of life and a chance to build emotional strength, you can reduce your fear of failure and increase your confidence and self-acceptance.

It is also important to remember that practicing emotional resilience is an ongoing process. It requires patience, self-compassion, and a willingness to confront uncomfortable emotions directly. Over time, by sitting with discomfort, understanding the temporary nature of emotions, and embracing vulnerability, you can develop a stronger sense of self and a more resilient emotional foundation.

NAVIGATING SEX AFTER A LONG-TERM RELATIONSHIP

Here's one of the most difficult and uncomfortable situations that can play on our insecurities. Re-entering the dating scene is a natural time for insecurities to surface. It involves adjusting to new dynamics, redefining expectations, and addressing any anxieties that may arise.

Practical Consideration

After a long-term relationship, you will need to address practical considerations that may have changed since you were last single. One of the most important aspects is using condoms and other forms of protection to prevent sexually transmitted infections (STIs) and unplanned pregnancies. Condoms may feel unfamiliar or interrupt the flow of intimacy, but they are crucial for ensuring safety and peace of mind.

Additionally, adjusting to new sexual scripts—what is expected, desired, and enjoyed in a sexual encounter—can take some time. Each new partner brings unique preferences and comfort levels, so it's vital to approach new experiences with an open mind and a willingness to learn. Managing expectations is also crucial. Rather than comparing new experiences to past ones, try to appreciate each moment for what it is without placing undue pressure on yourself or your partner.

Communication is Key

Open communication is the cornerstone of healthy sexual relationships, especially after leaving a long-term partnership. Discussing sex openly with new partners is the way to significantly reduce anxiety, build trust, and make the experience more enjoyable. It's important to express your needs, boundaries, and concerns honestly and listen to your partner's as well. Clear communication about sexual health, preferences, and expectations helps prevent misunderstandings and ensures that both of you feel comfortable and respected.

Have these conversations before becoming intimate to set the stage for a more relaxed and connected experience. The more openly you communicate, the easier it becomes to navigate any uncertainties or insecurities.

Throwing Out the Script

New relationships are an opportunity to throw out the old script and explore sex as a new experience. This might mean letting go of preconceived notions about what sex should look like or what roles each person should play. Instead, embrace a mindset of curiosity and experimentation, allowing for spontaneity and genuine connection. Being flexible and open to new ways of connecting can lead to more fulfilling and meaningful experiences. Whether trying new activities, exploring different forms of intimacy, or simply being present in the moment, throwing out the script encourages you to discover what truly feels good and authentic for you and your partner.

Although it can be fun, navigating sex after a long-term relationship is not always easy. It requires patience, openness, and a willingness to adapt. Focus on practical considerations, fostering clear communication, and being flexible with new experiences. That's how you can build fulfilling sexual relationships that honor both your past experiences and future possibilities.

Slow Down: Embracing the Unknown

When stepping back into the world of dating and intimacy after a long-term relationship, it's tempting to rush through the experience. You might feel pressure to prove yourself or assume that what worked in the past will work again. That thing you do with your tongue? It always worked before—so why wouldn't it now? The truth is, every person is different, and what felt right and natural with a previous partner might not translate to someone new.

Slowing down allows you to approach intimacy with curiosity rather than assumption. Instead of falling into old habits or relying on past experiences, take the time to explore what feels right with your new partner. Pay attention to their responses, ask questions, and be open to discovering what they enjoy. This isn't about proving what you know; it's about learning together.

Rushing through the process can create unnecessary pressure and leave both you and your partner feeling disconnected. Taking things slow fosters emotional connection, builds trust, and creates space for genuine pleasure to develop. It's okay not to have all the answers right away—allow yourself to enjoy the process of exploration without feeling like you need to have it all figured out.

TAKEAWAYS

Navigating male sexual insecurities involves a journey of self-acceptance, resilience, and redefining what it means to be masculine. Here's a breakdown of key concepts to consider:

- **Common Insecurities:** Many men face insecurities such as concerns about penis size, performance anxiety, and body image issues. These surface-level concerns often stem from deeper fears like the fear of rejection and losing connection with others. Understanding these underlying fears can help challenge the mindset of "I can't fuck this up" and help you realize your worth isn't tied to perfect sexual performance.
- **Embracing Insecurities:** Accepting insecurities doesn't mean ignoring or denying them. It's about leaning into discomfort and recognizing that vulnerability is a natural part of life.

- **Building Emotional Resilience:** Developing emotional resilience means becoming comfortable with discomfort rather than avoiding it. This involves acknowledging that emotions are temporary and learning to face difficult feelings without letting them control your self-perception.
- **Redefining Masculinity:** True confidence comes from within. Your value is not determined by meeting societal standards or fulfilling others' expectations. Adopting a more inclusive and compassionate view of masculinity encourages a more authentic and fulfilling sense of self.
- **The Ongoing Journey:** Building self-confidence and redefining masculinity requires continuous practice in acceptance and resilience. It involves embracing all parts of yourself, including vulnerabilities and imperfections. This allows you to foster more profound, more meaningful connections with yourself and others.

This is a journey that can lead you to redefine what it means to be masculine. It's a chance to move towards a broader, more inclusive understanding that values authenticity, empathy, and genuine connection over superficial measures of success. It's time to jettison the societal pressure and embrace self-worth.

CHAPTER TAKEAWAYS

- Addressing sexual insecurities fosters confidence and enjoyment.
- Reframing negative self-talk shifts focus toward personal strengths.
- Authenticity and vulnerability create more meaningful experiences.

CHAPTER 17

WHAT CAN I DO ABOUT PERFORMANCE ANXIETY?

It's that voice in your head that says, "What if I mess up?" or "What if I can't perform?" This anxiety can stem from past experiences, societal expectations, or even self-imposed pressure. Performance anxiety is one of the most common issues men bring up in my office, and it can be overwhelming. In fact, an estimated 9–25% of men experience sexual performance anxiety.[48]

Performance anxiety is an overwhelming pressure to "perform" perfectly in the bedroom, which often leads to stress and self-doubt rather than pleasure and connection. This kind of anxiety can stem from a range of psychological, social, and physical factors and often manifests in both emotional and physical symptoms. It can affect anyone, regardless of sexual experience or age, and is particularly prevalent among men due to societal pressures and myths about male sexuality. For the men I work with, performance anxiety is often keeping them from even enjoying sex the way they're body is designed to.

I've worked with men for whom performance anxiety kept them from being able to get an erection and men whose performance anxiety caused an inability to orgasm. But even mild performance anxiety can take you out of the moment, prevent your ability to connect with your partner, and dampen your enjoyment of sex.

---

[48] Pyke, R. E. (2020). Sexual performance anxiety. *Sexual Medicine Reviews, 8*(2), 183–190. https://doi.org/10.1016/j.sxmr.2019.07.001.

WHAT IS PERFORMANCE ANXIETY?

In simple terms, performance anxiety is the fear or worry of not being able to meet certain expectations during sex. It's driven by the thought that you're supposed to "perform" in a particular way, and if you don't, it will lead to disappointment, rejection, or humiliation. Unfortunately, this mindset can spiral out of control, leading to a lack of enjoyment, decreased sexual satisfaction, and even physical issues like erectile dysfunction or premature ejaculation.

Performance anxiety is not just in your head—it affects your body, too. The stress and fear that come with it can activate your body's fight-or-flight response, releasing stress hormones like adrenaline that interfere with the natural process of arousal. This creates a vicious cycle: the more you worry, the harder it becomes to relax, enjoy, and perform.

What's more, performance anxiety is a common cause of sexual dissatisfaction, and of dissatisfaction with relationships for both men and women (women have performance anxiety too, but we're here to talk about you). Understanding performance anxiety, and developing coping strategies, then, will strengthen your relationships and increase your sexual satisfaction.[49] Everybody wins. Let's dive in.

COMMON SYMPTOMS OF PERFORMANCE ANXIETY

Performance anxiety can manifest both physically and emotionally. The symptoms vary from person to person, but common signs include:

---

[49] Pyke, R. E. (2020). Sexual performance anxiety. *Sexual Medicine Reviews, 8*(2), 183–190. https://doi.org/10.1016/j.sxmr.2019.07.001.

WHAT CAN I DO ABOUT PERFORMANCE ANXIETY? 235

Physical Symptoms	Emotional Symptoms
Difficulty achieving or maintaining an erection	Overthinking every move or step during sexual activity
Premature ejaculation or delayed ejaculation	Fear of rejection or disappointing your partner
Rapid heartbeat	Feelings of inadequacy or embarrassment
Shortness of breath or shallow breathing	Loss of interest in sex due to fear of failure
Muscle tension, particularly in the pelvic region	Negative self-talk and self-criticism, such as "I'm not good enough" or "I'm going to fail again"
Excessive sweating	Avoiding sexual encounters altogether to prevent potential failure
Gastrointestinal discomfort (e.g., nausea, stomach cramps)	

Physical Symptoms:

- Difficulty achieving or maintaining an erection
- Premature ejaculation or delayed ejaculation
- Rapid heartbeat
- Shortness of breath or shallow breathing
- Muscle tension, particularly in the pelvic region
- Excessive sweating
- Gastrointestinal discomfort (e.g., nausea, stomach cramps)

Emotional Symptoms:

- Overthinking every move or step during sexual activity
- Fear of rejection or disappointing your partner
- Feelings of inadequacy or embarrassment
- Loss of interest in sex due to fear of failure
- Negative self-talk and self-criticism, such as "I'm not good enough" or "I'm going to fail again"
- Avoiding sexual encounters altogether to prevent potential failure

These symptoms can snowball over time. The more they occur, the more anxious you become about future encounters, creating a self-perpetuating cycle of stress and sexual dysfunction.

COMMON CAUSES OF PERFORMANCE ANXIETY

Performance anxiety doesn't come out of nowhere—it's usually a byproduct of various psychological, social, and physical factors.[50] Understanding these causes is key to managing and overcoming performance anxiety.

Psychological Factors

- **Stress and Anxiety Disorders:** General stress—whether it's work-related, financial, or personal—can easily spill over into the bedroom. Similarly, if you suffer from anxiety disorders, this underlying tension can be exacerbated by the pressure to

---

[50] McCabe, M. P. (2005). The role of performance anxiety in the development and maintenance of sexual dysfunction in men and women. *International Journal of Stress Management, 12*(4), 379–388. https://doi.org/10.1037/1072-5245.12.4.379.

perform sexually. When your mind is preoccupied with external worries or self-doubt, it becomes increasingly difficult to relax and enjoy the moment.
- **Low Self-Esteem and Negative Self-Talk:** The way you think about yourself plays a huge role in sexual performance. Men who suffer from low self-esteem or engage in negative self-talk are more likely to experience performance anxiety. Thoughts like "I'm not attractive enough" or "I'm not good in bed" can undermine confidence, making it harder to stay present during sex. This kind of thinking often leads to over focusing on technical aspects of performance (like staying erect or lasting long enough), which detracts from the enjoyment of the experience.
- **Past Traumatic Experiences:** Trauma, especially related to past sexual experiences, can significantly impact current sexual behavior. If you've had negative sexual encounters, been mocked, or felt shame in the past, these memories may resurface in new sexual situations, creating a barrier to fully engaging. Trauma can affect your body's response to arousal and heighten feelings of fear or inadequacy, making it difficult to feel comfortable and confident.

Social and Cultural Influences

- Society perpetuates the idea that men must always be sexually ready, rock-hard, and able to satisfy their partners without any hesitation. These myths are incredibly damaging because they create a standard that no one can consistently meet. The pressure to conform to these unrealistic ideals contributes significantly to performance anxiety, as men feel they must live up to these expectations or risk being seen as failures.
- Pornography often presents an exaggerated, unrealistic portrayal of sex, where actors perform with perfect bodies, lasting for extended periods without faltering. When people

compare their real life experiences to these idealized depictions, it can create feelings of inadequacy. The reality is that porn is designed to entertain, not educate, but its influence can lead many to develop distorted views of what "normal" sex should be like.
- It's common to feel pressure—real or imagined—from a partner to perform a certain way. If you believe that your partner has high expectations for your performance, it can increase anxiety. Even if your partner isn't explicitly putting pressure on you, your perception of what they might want or need can fuel your anxiety.

Physical and Medical Factors

- **Erectile Dysfunction (ED) and Premature Ejaculation (PE):** Both ED and PE are common medical conditions that can contribute to performance anxiety. Men with ED may worry about losing their erection mid-encounter, while those with PE may fear ejaculating too quickly. The more you focus on these concerns, the more likely it is they'll happen.
- **Medications and Substance Use:** Certain medications, such as antidepressants or drugs for high blood pressure, can interfere with sexual performance by reducing libido or making it more difficult to achieve an erection. Additionally, excessive alcohol or drug use can dampen your body's natural sexual responses, leading to underperformance and subsequent anxiety.
- **Lifestyle Choices:** Your overall health plays a huge role in sexual function. A poor diet, lack of exercise, insufficient sleep, and chronic stress can negatively affect your sexual health. For instance, not getting enough sleep can lead to fatigue and reduced libido, while poor nutrition can contribute to issues like ED. A sedentary lifestyle can also limit blood flow to the pelvic region, further exacerbating sexual performance issues.

MANAGING UNDERLYING EMOTIONAL ISSUES

One of the most important steps to overcoming performance anxiety is managing the emotional issues that contribute to it. Addressing the psychological roots of anxiety can help you break the cycle of fear and stress that impacts your sexual performance.

Mindful Mister Method

Mindfulness is a powerful tool for staying present and calming your mind. One of the primary techniques I recommend is the Mindful Mister Method. We discussed it in Chapter 1, but here's a review.

1. **Mindfulness (M):** *Check in with Your Emotions*
   - Before engaging in sex, it's important to recognize how your emotions impact your experience. Stress, unresolved conflicts, or fatigue can carry over into intimacy, making it difficult to be fully present. Taking a moment to assess and acknowledge your feelings allows you to enter the experience with greater awareness and connection.
2. **Intention (I):** *Stop the Spiral*
   - Many men experience intrusive thoughts and anxieties during sex, such as worrying about performance or comparing themselves to unrealistic standards. Setting an intention to stay focused on the present and reminding yourself why your partner is with you can help shift your mindset from self-doubt to self-assurance.
3. **Sensation (S):** *Slow it Down*
   - Rushing through sexual experiences can create a disconnection from pleasure. Slowing down your thoughts and focusing on breathing allows for greater bodily awareness. Tuning into sensations—such as touch, taste, and smell—helps you stay grounded and enhances the overall experience.

4. **Transformation (T):** *Shake It Off*
    - Intrusive thoughts are natural, but they don't have to control the experience. Practicing thought-stopping techniques and positive affirmations—such as reminding yourself that your partner is choosing to be with you—can help transform anxious energy into confidence and enjoyment.
5. **Embodiment (E):** *Bring Yourself Back*
    - Engaging with your senses fully immerses you in the moment. Focus on what you see, hear, touch, taste, and smell to enhance pleasure and connection. This step encourages you to embody the experience rather than analyze it, leading to deeper satisfaction.
6. **Reflection (R):** *Appreciation, Connection, Gratitude*
    - After intimacy, taking time to reflect on the experience can strengthen your connection with your partner. Expressing gratitude and acknowledging what felt good—both emotionally and physically—helps foster a deeper sense of appreciation and connection moving forward.

Some Other Ideas to Try

- **Deep Breathing:** Start by taking slow, deep breaths in through your nose and out through your mouth. Focus on the rise and fall of your chest or belly. As you breathe, allow yourself to notice how your body feels without judgment.
- **Progressive Muscle Relaxation:** Begin by tensing, then relaxing different muscle groups, starting from your toes and working your way up to your head. This helps relieve physical tension, which can enhance relaxation and enjoyment during sex.
- **Cognitive Behavioral Therapy (CBT):** CBT is an evidence-based therapy that helps you challenge and change negative thought patterns. In the context of performance anxiety,

CBT can help you identify unhelpful beliefs, like "I need to last a certain amount of time" or "I'm going to fail," and replace them with more realistic and affirming thoughts, such as "I'm here to connect, not perform." Over time, this can reduce the fear and pressure you feel during sexual encounters.

- **Challenging Negative Self-Talk:** Pay attention to the things you say to yourself during sex. Are you putting yourself down, or are you too focused on what could go wrong? Practice interrupting these negative thoughts and reframing them in a more compassionate light. For example, instead of thinking, "I can't keep it up," remind yourself, "This is about connection, not perfection. My partner is with me because they want to be."
- **Improving Communication With Your Partner:** Being open with your partner about your feelings and fears can significantly reduce anxiety. Share your worries, and you may find that your partner is more understanding and supportive than you imagined. You don't need to carry the burden of performance alone—your partner is part of the equation, and open communication will help you feel more connected and less pressured.
- **Addressing the Physical Side:** Addressing the physical aspects of performance anxiety is just as important as managing the emotional ones. Improving your lifestyle, health, and sexual habits can greatly enhance your ability to enjoy sex without anxiety.
- **Prioritize Health:** Make sure you're eating well, exercising regularly, and getting enough sleep. A healthy body supports a healthy sexual response. Exercise, in particular, increases blood flow and boosts your mood, both of which can improve sexual performance.
- **Address Medical Issues:** If you suspect that a medical condition or medication is contributing to your anxiety, talk to your doctor. Conditions like ED or PE are common, and there are treatments available. You don't need to suffer in silence.

THE PRESSURE MEN PUT ON THEMSELVES

When it comes to sexual performance, the pressure men place on themselves can often be even greater than any external expectations. This self-imposed pressure stems from a mix of personal insecurities, societal messaging, and deeply ingrained beliefs about what it means to be a man. The internalized expectation to always "perform" at peak levels can create a cycle of anxiety, self-doubt, and even avoidance of intimacy.

The Expectation to Always "Be Ready"

Men are often conditioned to believe they should always be in the mood, ready to perform, and capable of satisfying their partners effortlessly. The cultural message that "real men" have high sex drives and endless stamina leads many to feel inadequate when their reality doesn't align with these unrealistic standards. If desire fluctuates, or if an erection doesn't happen on cue, men may interpret it as a failure rather than a natural response to stress, fatigue, or relationship dynamics.

What this Pressure Looks Like:

- Feeling ashamed if you're not always in the mood.
- Believing you should never say "no" to sex.
- Worrying that your partner will be disappointed if you can't perform on demand.

Measuring Up to Past Experiences

Many men compare their current sexual experiences to their past ones—whether it's a previous relationship, a "better" time in their life, or even past moments with their current partner. This can create an unrealistic benchmark that ignores the reality that bodies and relationships change over time. Clinging to the idea that sex must always match a previous high point can result in performance anxiety and feelings of inadequacy when expectations aren't met.

How this Pressure Manifests:

- Constantly comparing performance to younger years or peak experiences.
- Feeling pressure to recreate "perfect" moments instead of enjoying what's happening now.
- Trying too hard to please instead of focusing on mutual enjoyment.

The Perfectionist Mindset

Many men approach sex with a perfectionist mindset—believing they need to get everything right, from technique and stamina to their partner's satisfaction. This all-or-nothing thinking can make it difficult to enjoy intimacy because the focus is placed on meeting an imaginary standard rather than being present. The fear of making mistakes or not living up to perceived expectations can make sexual encounters feel more like a test than an opportunity for connection.

Signs of Perfectionist Pressure:

- Obsessing over technique and worrying if you're "doing it right."
- Feeling like sex needs to be an intense performance every time.
- Avoiding intimacy for fear of falling short.

Fear of Judgment and Rejection

Even if a partner hasn't expressed any dissatisfaction, many men worry about being judged for their sexual performance. This fear can lead to avoidance behaviors, such as declining sex altogether or sticking to "safe" routines that don't challenge comfort zones. The internal dialogue often centers around a fear of not being good enough, being perceived as lacking experience, or not measuring up to a partner's expectations.

Common Fears Include:

- "What if I can't satisfy my partner?"
- "What if I don't last long enough?"
- "What if they've been with someone better?"

HOW TO RELEASE THE PRESSURE

Letting go of self-imposed expectations is key to reducing performance anxiety and fostering a more fulfilling sex life. Some ways to achieve this include:

- **Shift the Focus to Connection:** Remind yourself that sex is about intimacy and connection, not performance. Engage with your partner emotionally and enjoy the moment rather than aiming for perfection.
- **Challenge Unrealistic Expectations:** Recognize and dismantle unrealistic beliefs about what sex should look like. No one is perfect in bed every time, and your worth isn't defined by your performance.
- **Embrace Vulnerability:** It's okay to admit fears and uncertainties to your partner. Being open about your feelings can help create a more supportive and understanding sexual relationship.
- **Practice Self-Compassion:** Treat yourself with the same kindness you would offer a friend. Acknowledge that performance anxiety is common and doesn't define your masculinity or self-worth.

By recognizing the pressure you place on yourself and actively working to release it, you can create a more relaxed and enjoyable approach to sex—one that values authenticity and connection over unrealistic expectations.

> **CHAPTER TAKEAWAYS**
>
> - Mindfulness techniques help stay present and enjoy intimacy.
> - Anxiety disrupts arousal, but reframing thoughts improves experience.
> - A focus on pleasure over performance eases pressure and enhances connection.

PART 4

Mindful Sex for Life

CHAPTER 18

WHAT IS SENSATE FOCUS?

Sensate Focus is a therapeutic method developed in the 1960s by sex researchers Masters and Johnson to help couples reduce performance anxiety and improve their emotional and physical connection. It's a practice involving a series of structured, non-demanding touch exercises designed to shift the focus from achieving specific sexual outcomes to fully experiencing the present moment. It encourages mindfulness and present moment awareness during sexual encounters, helping people reconnect with their bodies and each other.[51]

The primary goal of Sensate Focus is to alleviate the pressure to perform during sexual activity, whether that's related to achieving orgasm or pleasing a partner. This reduction in performance anxiety creates a space for more natural, relaxed interactions. Instead of focusing on expectations, you can learn to explore sensations, touch, and emotional connection with a sense of curiosity and openness. This approach helps you and your partner build trust, enhance communication, and ultimately experience greater satisfaction in your intimate lives.

Therefore, in this chapter, we will explore what Sensate Focus is, how to adjust your focus, and how you can incorporate Sensate Focus into your relationships through a step-by-step guide. So, let's get started.

---

[51] Masters, W. H., Johnson, V. E., Kolodny, R. C., & Cornell Health. (1994). Sensate focus. In *Heterosexuality* (pp. 25–41). HarperCollins.

SHIFTING FROM PERFORMANCE TO PLEASURE AND CONNECTION

Sensate Focus is a method to move away from performance-based anxiety and toward experiencing pleasure and connection in your sexual relationships. The goal is to focus on non-demanding touch and mindfulness. You and your partner strive to be fully present in the moment, exploring sensations rather than striving for specific sexual outcomes like orgasm.

One of the key benefits of Sensate Focus is its ability to shift attention away from the pressure to perform and allow you to focus on enjoying the physical and emotional aspects of intimacy. This approach reduces anxiety, builds trust, and deepens the bond between you and your partner by fostering a more relaxed, connected experience.

Mindfulness also plays a central role, as it encourages you to remain aware of your sensations and emotions during intimate moments. By staying grounded in the present, you and your partner can experience greater satisfaction and connection, making your sexual encounters more fulfilling and less stressful.

MOVING BEYOND JUDGMENT

In intimate moments, shifting from judgment and evaluation to simply "being" and "experiencing" can profoundly enhance your connection. Instead of assessing or analyzing each touch, strive to fully immerse yourself in the experience. Focus on the physical sensations as they unfold, without adding layers of judgment or expectation.

Pay attention to the qualities of your partner's skin—notice if it feels smooth, rough, warm, or moist. This approach encourages a more mindful engagement with each sensation, allowing you to appreciate the moment without the distraction of evaluation. Concentrating on the sensory experience rather than preconceived notions or goals fosters a deeper connection and more genuine enjoyment of the physical and emotional interactions.

SENSUALITY VS. SEXUALITY

When practicing Sensate Focus, it's essential to distinguish between sensuality and sexuality. Set the stage for sensuality rather than sexuality by clearly defining boundaries. During your sensual experience, avoid engaging in any sexual activities such as touching genitals or breasts, oral sex, or intercourse. This "prohibition" helps maintain a clear focus on sensual touch as a distinct and valuable experience in its own right.

This approach removes any pressure for you or your partner to respond in a specific way, which can often accompany sexual activities. By setting these boundaries, you create a space where both of you can explore and enjoy the sensual side of touch without the expectations or ingrained behavior patterns that can influence sex. Many couples find that dedicating time to this process reawakens their sensual and sexual feelings in a refreshing and meaningful way.

To make the most of these exercises, strive for an experience where both of you are relaxed, rested, and in a kind and open state of mind. Privacy is crucial, so choose a quiet, uninterrupted setting and allocate time, maybe 30 to 40 minutes, for the practice. Although nudity is ideal for unimpeded skin-to-skin contact, if that's not feasible, opt for loose, comfortable clothing to minimize any constrictions. This preparation allows you to fully engage in the Sensate Focus process and discover new dimensions of sensuality together.

WHO CAN BENEFIT FROM SENSATE FOCUS?

Sensate Focus can be a valuable tool for a wide range of people, particularly those facing sexual difficulties or feeling disconnected in their relationships. Couples who experience challenges such as reduced intimacy, lack of sexual satisfaction, or emotional distance may find that Sensate Focus helps them reconnect both physically and emotionally. Emphasizing touch and presence over performance creates a safe space for rebuilding trust and intimacy.

This method is also beneficial for those who struggle with performance anxiety during sex. The pressure to achieve specific outcomes, like orgasm or pleasing a partner, can create stress and detract from the experience. Sensate Focus alleviates this by encouraging a focus on sensations and connection, rather than performance.

While Sensate Focus is not a one-size-fits-all solution, it has proven effective for many. Its flexibility allows you to tailor the process to your unique needs, making it a versatile approach to improving sexual satisfaction and deepening relationships.

THE IMPORTANCE OF SHIFTING YOUR FOCUS

Performance-based expectations in sexual relationships can have a significant negative impact on satisfaction and intimacy. When you focus too much on achieving specific outcomes, such as reaching orgasm or ensuring your partner's satisfaction, the pressure to "perform" can create stress and anxiety. This performance mindset often leads to feelings of inadequacy or disappointment, diminishing the overall enjoyment of the experience.

By shifting the focus from performance to pleasure, you can reduce this pressure and engage more fully in the moment. Instead of worrying about achieving specific results, you can concentrate on the sensations, emotions, and connection you feel with your partner. This change in focus encourages a deeper sense of relaxation and enjoyment, enhancing the quality of your intimate encounters. Focusing on pleasure and connection rather than outcomes allows you to experience sex as a more spontaneous and fulfilling activity.

THE ROLE OF MINDFULNESS IN SENSATE FOCUS

Mindfulness plays a crucial role in Sensate Focus by enhancing awareness of sensations and emotions during intimate encounters. It is the method you can use to practice staying present in the moment. By practicing mindfulness, you and your partner can better attune themselves to the physical sensations of touch, as well as the emotional responses that arise.

The connection between mindfulness and sexual satisfaction is profound. When you focus on the present moment, you can let go of performance anxiety and expectations, leading to a more relaxed and enjoyable experience. Mindfulness allows you to explore your partner's body with a sense of curiosity and openness rather than being preoccupied with achieving specific outcomes. This shift in focus is about finding authentic pleasure.

To stay present and engaged during sexual encounters, several techniques can be employed.

- Deep breathing helps ground you in the moment, reducing stress and enhancing focus on physical sensations.
- Grounding techniques, such as consciously feeling the texture of your partner's skin or noticing the warmth of their touch, can also aid in maintaining mindfulness.

By integrating these practices into their intimate moments, couples can create a more fulfilling and connected sexual experience.

THE MULTISTEP PROCESS OF SENSATE FOCUS

Once we understand the mindful, non-judgmental, sensual approach of Sensate Focus, we are ready to engage in this connection of pleasure and intimacy. So, let's look at ways to incorporate it into your life through a step-by-step process.

Step 1: Preparing for Sensate Focus

- **Setting the Stage:** Creating a safe and comfortable environment is key to the success of Sensate Focus exercises. The setting should encourage relaxation and minimize distractions, allowing both partners to focus fully on the experience. This can involve dimming the lights, playing calming music, and ensuring that the space is private and free from interruptions. Setting aside uninterrupted time is essential, as the exercises require full attention and a sense of security to foster openness and connection.
- **Communicating With Your Partner:** Introducing the concept of Sensate Focus to your partner is a critical first step. It's important to explain that the goal is to reduce pressure and foster intimacy through mindful touch, rather than performance. Openly discussing your mutual goals, setting expectations, and establishing boundaries will help ensure both you and your partner feel comfortable. Since the initial exercises are non-sexual, they can help relieve any performance pressure and create a relaxed atmosphere for both of you.
- **Establishing Boundaries and Guidelines:** Before beginning Sensate Focus, establish clear boundaries for each session. Discuss which areas of the body are comfortable for touch, and emphasize the importance of consent at every stage. Partners should check in with each other before, during, and after each session to ensure that both feel at ease. Sensate Focus is about the process, not the outcome, so the goal of orgasm should be set aside in the early stages. This allows you and your partner to focus on the sensations and the shared experience.

Step 2: Non-Sexual Touch

- **Focusing on Non-Sexual Touch:** In the first stage of Sensate Focus, the focus is exclusively on non-sexual touch.

Explore touch in a mindful, relaxed manner, noticing the textures, temperatures, and pressure of each touch. Mindfulness plays a key role in this process. Stay present by focusing on the sensory experience rather than any sexual outcome. Remember the techniques such as deep breathing and grounding that can help you maintain focus, reduce distractions, and enhance awareness.

- **Exercises:** To begin, take turns engaging in gentle, non-sexual touch. This might involve light stroking, firm pressure, or simply resting a hand on your partner's skin. The aim is to explore different types of touch and observe how each feels. It's important to avoid sexual areas during this stage to remove any pressure to perform or achieve arousal. You and your partner can switch roles, taking time to touch and be touched, while reflecting on your sensations and emotions. Questions like, "How do I feel during this touch?" or "What sensations am I noticing?" can help foster self-awareness and reflection during and after the exercises.
- **Building Trust and Connection:** During this practice, strive to develop emotional and physical trust with your partner. By engaging in this non-demanding, non-sexual touch, you can create a safe space where you can explore each other's bodies without expectation. Open communication is vital throughout, as it helps both of you express your feelings and adjust the experience as needed. This foundation of trust and connection allows you and your partner to deepen your intimacy in a mindful way without pressure.

Step 3: Moving to More Intimate Touch

- **Introducing More Intimate Touch:** Begin to progress from non-sexual touch to more intimate forms of contact, while still avoiding direct genital stimulation. The focus remains on exploring each other's bodies in a way that feels good, rather than adhering to any expectations or goals. During this stage, expand the areas of the body you touch, paying attention to sensations of warmth, texture, and pressure. Mindfulness remains essential, with both you and your partner staying present in the moment and prioritizing connection over arousal.

- **Exercises:** This stage involves guided exercises where you can gently explore more intimate areas. For instance, touch might include areas like the chest or inner thighs, but always with a focus on curiosity and mutual consent. The goal is not to rush into sexual touch but to enjoy the process of discovery and connection. Maintaining a relaxed, open atmosphere is key to reducing pressure. Continue to avoid the expectation of orgasm or any specific outcome.
- **Reflecting on Progress:** As you and your partner move through this stage, reflection becomes an important part of the process. It's a good time to assess your comfort levels, emotional connection, and any shifts in your feelings of intimacy or satisfaction. Reflection questions like, "How do I feel about the more intimate touch?" or "How does this experience differ from previous sexual interactions?" can help guide the conversation. Openly discussing the evolving experience can deepen trust and highlight the progress made in building a stronger emotional and physical connection.

Step 4: Genital Touch

- **Incorporating Genital Touch:** In this stage, introduce gentle and mindful genital touch, continuing to emphasize sensation over arousal. The goal is to maintain the mindfulness and presence developed in earlier stages, focusing on how the touch feels rather than any expectations around sexual performance or orgasm. It's crucial for both you and your partner to remain attuned to each other.

- **Exercises:** In this stage, you can begin to explore genital touch with the same attention to sensations you've practiced before. Starting with a gentle touch and progressing at a comfortable pace, maintain the focus on connection rather than rushing toward sexual activity. Different types of touch—varying speed, pressure, and rhythm—can be explored to discover what feels good for you and your partner. Stay present and resist the urge to move into more conventional sexual activities prematurely. This will deepen the experience, keeping the emphasis on mutual pleasure and intimacy.
- **Deepening Emotional Intimacy:** This stage is not just about increasing physical intimacy. It also provides an opportunity to deepen emotional intimacy and trust between you and your partner. As a couple, engage in this mindful and intentional touch to feel more connected emotionally and physically. Reflecting on how this process has shifted your perceptions of sex and intimacy can foster a greater sense of closeness, making the experience of shared pleasure more fulfilling.

Step 5: Integrating Sensate Focus Into Your Sex Life

- **Transitioning to Full Sexual Activity:** Once you and your partner are comfortable with the exercises, it may be time to transition from Sensate Focus to full sexual activity. The key is to carry the mindfulness, presence, and connection developed during the exercises into more conventional sexual encounters. Focus on pleasure and communication rather than performance or outcomes and continue to experience sex as a deeply intimate and enjoyable activity.
- **Overcoming Common Challenges:** As with any process, there may be challenges or setbacks. Performance anxiety might resurface, or discomfort with certain exercises could arise. If this

happens, it's helpful to return to earlier stages of Sensate Focus, where there is less pressure and more time for reflection and adjustment. If difficulties persist, seeking professional guidance from a therapist or sexual health expert can offer additional support and strategies.
- **Making Sensate Focus a Regular Practice:** To keep the connection strong, Sensate Focus can be integrated into your regular sexual routine. Using these exercises as a tool to maintain and enhance sexual intimacy encourages ongoing growth in your relationship.

BUILDING TRUST AND INTIMACY WITH SENSATE FOCUS

As you follow this step-by-step guide to practicing Sensate Focus, you discover more than a thriving sex life. You can find that it builds trust and intimacy throughout your relationship.

Sensate Focus is a powerful tool for building trust and intimacy, particularly for those affected by sexual difficulties or emotional disconnection. The practice fosters emotional safety by creating a non-judgmental space where you and your partner can explore each other's bodies and feelings without the pressure to perform. This safe environment encourages open communication and mutual respect, laying the groundwork for deeper emotional trust.

For couples dealing with sexual difficulties, Sensate Focus provides a structured approach to reconnecting. By shifting the focus away from specific outcomes and towards the enjoyment of touch and presence, you can address underlying issues in a supportive and gentle manner, which can be transformative for relationships struggling with intimacy issues.

The long-term impact of incorporating Sensate Focus into a relationship is significant. As you and your partner continue to practice mindfulness and non-demanding touch, you build a stronger emotional bond and a more satisfying sexual connection. This ongoing process of exploration and communication enhances overall intimacy, creating a deeper, more resilient connection. Through consistent practice, you can cultivate a lasting sense of closeness and satisfaction in your relationship.

ADAPTING SENSATE FOCUS TO YOUR RELATIONSHIP

One of the strengths of Sensate Focus is its flexibility. It can be tailored to fit your unique needs. The method is designed to adapt to various comfort levels, preferences, and progress, making it a versatile tool for enhancing intimacy and connection.

As you adapt your practice of Sensate Focus, patience, and open communication are crucial. It's important to approach the practice with a willingness to adjust and evolve based on your experience and feedback from your partner.

This personalized approach allows for a more gradual and supportive experience, ensuring that Sensate Focus serves as a positive and enriching part of your relationship.

TAKEAWAYS

Senate Focus can be a powerful tool in your sex life and intimacy with your partner. It is a deep, emotional, and sensual process. So, let's review the things we have covered in this chapter.

- **Understanding Sensate Focus:** Sensate Focus is a therapeutic technique designed to shift attention from performance-based goals to experiencing pleasure and connection. Originating from sex therapy research, it aims to reduce performance anxiety and promote a deeper emotional and physical bond between partners. By fostering present moment awareness, Sensate Focus helps you engage more fully in your sexual encounters.

- **Who Can Benefit:** Sensate Focus is beneficial for a wide range of people, including those experiencing sexual difficulties, performance anxiety, or seeking to build trust and intimacy. While it is not a one-size-fits-all solution, its adaptable nature makes it effective for many people, offering a flexible approach to enhancing sexual satisfaction and connection.
- **Shifting Focus from Performance to Pleasure:** Performance-based expectations, such as achieving orgasm or satisfying a partner, can create stress and detract from sexual enjoyment. By focusing on pleasure, sensations, and connection, Sensate Focus helps alleviate this pressure, leading to a more fulfilling and relaxed sexual experience.
- **The Role of Mindfulness:** Mindfulness is integral to Sensate Focus, enhancing awareness of physical sensations and emotional responses. Techniques such as deep breathing and grounding help you stay present, which is crucial for deepening sexual satisfaction and maintaining engagement in the moment.
- **The Multistep Process:** Sensate Focus gradually progresses from non-demanding touch to more intimate interactions. This step-by-step approach encourages partners to focus on sensual touch, emphasizing communication and mutual consent throughout the process.
- **Building Trust and Intimacy:** The practice of Sensate Focus fosters emotional safety and trust between partners. It is particularly beneficial for relationships facing sexual difficulties, as it helps build a stronger, more intimate connection over time. The long-term impact includes a deeper emotional bond and enhanced overall intimacy.
- **Adapting to Your Relationship:** Sensate Focus is designed to be flexible, allowing it to be adapted to fit your needs.

Patience and open communication are key, as partners tailor the practice based on comfort levels and progress. This personalized approach ensures that Sensate Focus remains a supportive and enriching part of your relationship.

With these guidelines, you can begin a conversation with your partner and enjoy the sensual relationship you desire.

CHAPTER TAKEAWAYS

- Engaging fully in sensation enhances sexual connection.
- Mindfulness practices improve pleasure and reduce anxiety.
- Sensate focus techniques strengthen intimacy and awareness.

CHAPTER 19

WHAT DO I REALLY CARE ABOUT WHEN IT COMES TO SEX?

Core values play a pivotal role in shaping behaviors, preferences, and boundaries within your sexual relationships. They act as a compass, guiding how you navigate intimate interactions and the choices you make regarding your sexual health. When your values are clear and aligned with your actions, you experience more fulfilling and harmonious relationships.

Conversely, misaligned values can lead to confusion, dissatisfaction, and conflict. For instance, if your core value is honesty but you engage in deceptive behaviors, this misalignment can cause emotional distress. Imagine someone who values respect and equality in relationships but finds themselves in a situation where their partner consistently disregards these principles. This misalignment can lead to significant emotional turmoil and a need to reevaluate their relationship choices.

IDENTIFYING YOUR CORE VALUES

To build healthier relationships, it's crucial to identify your core values that guide your decisions and behaviors. Here is an activity to make it easy to get started.

- **Step 1: Create a Values List**
  Begin by creating a comprehensive list of values related to your personal and sexual health. These might include values like

respect, honesty, intimacy, consent, and trust. Reflect on each value and its relevance in your life. How does it influence your sexual interactions? This process helps in understanding what principles are most important to you and how they impact your choices. To help, here is a list of common core values.

> Authenticity, Balance, Bravery, Compassion, Confidence, Connection, Contribution, Cooperation, Courage, Creativity, Curiosity, Dependability, Determination, Empathy, Equality, Excellence, Fairness, Faith, Freedom, Generosity, Gratitude, Growth, Honesty, Humility, Inclusion, Independence, Integrity, Joy, Justice, Kindness, Leadership, Learning, Loyalty, Mindfulness, Open-mindedness, Optimism, Patience, Respect, Responsibility, Wisdom.

- **Step 2: Narrowing Down Your Top Five Values**
  After listing potential values, focus on narrowing them down to your top five. This exercise helps simplify decision-making and ensures consistency in your actions. For example, if "honesty" is one of your top values, it will influence how you communicate about your needs and boundaries in sexual relationships. These key values can help you make clearer, more consistent decisions that align with your core beliefs.
- **Step 3: Reflecting on Your Values**
  Once you've identified your core values, reflect on the significance. Consider how each chosen value influences your decisions and behaviors in your sexual life. Reflect on past experiences where these values were particularly relevant or tested. If "consent" is a core value, think about how this principle has guided your interactions and helped you maintain healthy boundaries.
- **Step 4: Real Life Applications of Core Values**
  Understanding how values guide your behavior and decision-making can be enlightening. Let's think about

"intimacy" as a core value. It may lead you to prioritize deep emotional connections in your relationships, ensuring that your sexual experiences are meaningful and fulfilling.

Reflective questions can help you explore this further, so let's think through these:

- How do my values shape my sexual relationships?
- In what ways do they guide my behavior and choices?
- What personal stories or scenarios do I have where living in alignment with my values had a positive impact?

Answering questions like these leads to real life applications. Let's take "trust" as an example. If someone values trust, they might find their relationships are stronger and more satisfying when they are open and honest about their desires and boundaries.

THE IMPORTANCE OF VALUES IN SEXUAL HEALTH

Core values are not just abstract ideals. They are the foundational beliefs that guide your actions and decisions, especially in intimate contexts. Exploring how these values shape your experiences, influence your choices, and align with your true self can help you understand the profound impact they have on your sexual satisfaction and overall well-being.

Why Values Matter

These values guide decisions about what feels right or wrong in a sexual context. So, let's analyze a few of the areas of impact.

- Fundamental Beliefs: Core values are the fundamental beliefs that guide your actions and decisions. They act as a moral compass, providing a framework through which we view the world and make choices. In sexual health, these values are especially important as they dictate how we approach intimacy, relationships, and personal boundaries.

- Shaping Experiences: Our core values significantly influence our sexual experiences and choices. These principles will guide how you interact with your partner and make decisions about sexual activities. This influence ensures that your sexual experiences are aligned with what feels right and meaningful to you.
- Alignment With True Self: When you align your sexual decisions with your core values, you ensure that your actions reflect your true self. This alignment means that your sexual behavior is consistent with your inner beliefs and convictions, leading to a more authentic and fulfilling experience.
- Greater Satisfaction: Aligning your actions with your values leads to greater satisfaction by reducing internal conflict. When your choices match your beliefs, you avoid feelings of guilt or regret, fostering a sense of consistency in your life. This consistency enhances your overall well-being and satisfaction with your sexual experiences.
- Consistency and Integrity: Making choices that reflect your deepest beliefs creates integrity in your actions. When your behavior is aligned with your core values, it demonstrates a commitment to living authentically. This integrity reinforces your self-respect and strengthens your sense of moral coherence.
- Self-Respect and Confidence: The consistency between your values and actions nurtures self-respect and confidence. Knowing that you are living in accordance with your deepest beliefs supports a more fulfilling sexual life. It empowers you to engage in relationships and activities that genuinely resonate with who you are, enhancing both your self-esteem and personal satisfaction.

IMPACT ON SEXUAL RELATIONSHIPS

Making choices that reflect your fundamental beliefs creates a more satisfying connection with your partner. This alignment often leads to relationships that are more aligned with your true self and your partner's, fostering greater overall happiness. Here are some specific ways that values will impact your sexual relationships:

- Respectful and Consensual Interactions: Values-driven choices naturally lead to more respectful and consensual interactions. If mutual respect and consent are core values for you, your actions will likely ensure that you and your partner feel valued and heard. This approach fosters an environment where you are both comfortable and enthusiastic about your interactions, leading to more fulfilling experiences.
- Preventing Regret and Guilt: Aligning your actions with your values helps avoid feelings of regret and guilt. When your behavior is consistent with your beliefs, you avoid the internal conflict that arises from acting against your principles. This alignment ensures that you feel at peace with your decisions, reducing the likelihood of negative emotions that can arise from misalignment.
- Enhanced Trust and Communication: Living in accordance with your values strengthens trust and communication with your partner. You will naturally communicate more openly, which fosters a deeper level of trust. This honest communication lays the groundwork for a stronger and more understanding relationship.
- Strong Foundations: Clear, honest intentions rooted in your core beliefs create a solid foundation for meaningful and enduring connections. When you share similar values and communicate your intentions clearly, it sets the stage for a relationship

built on mutual respect and understanding. This strong foundation supports long-term satisfaction and stability in the relationship.

CONNECTION BETWEEN LIVING AUTHENTICALLY AND SEXUAL SATISFACTION

Living authentically involves ensuring that your actions, desires, and boundaries are in harmony with your inner beliefs and values. When you act in ways that reflect your true self, you create a more genuine and fulfilling connection. So, here are some of the benefits of this authentic living:

- Reducing External Pressure: Authenticity helps you resist the pressure to conform to external expectations or societal norms that may not align with your true self. When you remain true to your own values, you are less influenced by what others think or expect. This freedom allows you to make choices that are genuinely right for you rather than simply following popular trends or pressures.
- Genuine Satisfaction: When you stay true to your values, you engage in sexual activities and relationships that genuinely satisfy you. Authenticity ensures that your sexual life resonates with your true desires, enhancing overall satisfaction.
- Enriched Sexual Experiences: Aligning your actions with your core values enriches your sexual experiences and contributes to your overall well-being. When your sexual life reflects your authentic self, you are more likely to experience deeper connections and pleasure. This alignment supports a more rewarding and emotionally satisfying sexual life.
- Freedom to Explore: Being authentic provides the freedom to explore and enjoy your sexuality in ways that feel right for you.

When you embrace your true self, you have the confidence to explore new experiences that align with your values and desires. This freedom enhances personal satisfaction and fulfillment, allowing you to fully embrace and enjoy your sexual life.

APPLYING YOUR VALUES IN SEXUAL RELATIONSHIPS

Navigating sexual relationships with integrity involves applying your core values to various scenarios of life, from new connections to established partnerships. Clear communication of your values can set the foundation for healthy relationships. It can help you handle conflicts in a way that respects your principles. Values can guide you to explore new desires while staying true to your core beliefs. Incorporating your core values into these aspects of your sexual life can ensure that your interactions are respectful, fulfilling, and aligned with your authentic self. Let's delve into some practical approaches for applying your values to build stronger and more satisfying relationships.

Scenario 1: Navigating New Relationships

When entering a new relationship, clear communication of your core values is essential for building a solid foundation. Start by having an open conversation with your partner about what is important to you.

Consider a scenario where you value "honesty" and "consent." As you start a new relationship, you might say to your partner, "I believe in open communication and respecting each other's boundaries. It's important to me that we discuss our expectations and check in with each other regularly to ensure we're both comfortable and on the same page."

This proactive approach helps establish mutual understanding and sets the stage for a respectful, values-aligned relationship.

Scenario 2: Addressing Conflict in Established Relationships

Relationships take work. Conflict is inevitable in any relationship, but how you navigate it can significantly impact the health and longevity of your connection. You can use your core values as a guide for resolving disagreements and working to improve your relationships.

When addressing a disagreement, practice active listening and express your feelings using "I" statements, such as "I feel upset when . . ." This approach ensures that you communicate your concerns without placing blame. Look for compromises that honor core values as well as those of your partner.

Scenario 3: Exploring New Sexual Desires

Exploring new sexual experiences can be exciting, but it's important to balance this with respect for your values and boundaries. Communicate with your partner about your desires and ensure these conversations align with your values.

If you're interested in trying a new sexual activity, discuss it with your partner in a way that reflects your values. You might say, "I've been thinking about exploring something new, and I want to make sure we're both comfortable and excited about it. Let's talk about how we can make this experience enjoyable for both of us."

It's crucial to prioritize safety and consent. Make sure that both you and your partner are entirely comfortable and enthusiastic about any new experiences. Establish clear boundaries and check in with each other regularly to ensure that the exploration remains consensual and enjoyable.

Applying your values to these scenarios creates a framework for healthier, more fulfilling sexual relationships. Whether navigating new relationships, addressing conflicts, or exploring new desires, staying true to your core values fosters respect, understanding, and mutual satisfaction.

COMMITMENT TO LIVING YOUR VALUES

Decisions have to be made and those decisions may need to be adjusted over time. Living your values means consistently aligning your actions and decisions with your core beliefs, even as life evolves. This dedication ensures that your behavior in relationships and sexual experiences reflects what is important, fostering authenticity and integrity. You create a solid foundation for personal growth and fulfilling connections.

This ongoing commitment enhances your self-respect and satisfaction. Also, it strengthens your relationships, as both you and your partners can trust that your actions are guided by a clear set of principles. Regularly revisiting and refining your values helps maintain this alignment and ensures that your decisions continue to resonate with your evolving self.

CREATING A PERSONAL VALUES STATEMENT

Crafting a Personal Values Statement is a powerful way to solidify this commitment. This is a concise summary of your guiding principles, helping you stay aligned with what is most important to you. To create your statement, return to your reflections on your core values and how they influence your behavior. Based on these reflections, write a clear, affirming declaration that outlines your commitment.

For example, your Personal Values Statement might read: "I am committed to maintaining honesty, respect, and mutual consent in all my sexual relationships. These values guide my interactions and decisions, ensuring that I build connections based on trust and open communication."

This statement can be a guide for making decisions and navigating relationships, keeping you grounded in your core beliefs.

COMMUNICATION ABOUT YOUR VALUES

Talking about your sexual values with your partner is all about being clear, straightforward, and honest. Start by laying it out in a way that shows what matters to you—whether it's trust, respect, or keeping things fun and adventurous. A good way to approach it is by saying what's important to you and why, then giving your partner space to do the same. Being upfront about your expectations and boundaries helps avoid misunderstandings and keeps things solid between you both. It's not about overcomplicating things—just being real about what works for you and what doesn't.

Sentence Starters:

1. "For me, having trust and honesty in our sex life is key because it helps me feel more connected and comfortable with you."
2. "I really value open communication when it comes to sex, and I'd love for us to be able to talk about what we both enjoy and need."
3. "One thing that's important to me is mutual respect in the bedroom—I want to make sure we're always on the same page and both feeling good about what we're doing."

LONG-TERM BENEFITS OF LIVING ACCORDING TO YOUR VALUES

Living in alignment with your values can profoundly impact various aspects of your life. Adhering to your core values often leads to greater satisfaction, improved relationship quality, and enhanced overall well-being. When your actions reflect your values, you are more likely to experience fulfilling, harmonious relationships and a deeper sense of self-respect.

Testimonies from those who have integrated their values into their sexual lives often highlight the positive changes they've experienced, such as increased trust and emotional connection with their partners.

It's also important to recognize that your values might shift or require re-evaluation as life circumstances and relationships evolve. Regularly revisiting and revising your Personal Values Statement can help you stay aligned with your evolving beliefs and ensure that your actions continue to reflect what is most important to you. This ongoing commitment to living according to your values supports long-term satisfaction and personal growth in your sexual relationships.

TAKEAWAYS

If you take nothing else from this chapter, understand that knowing yourself is the key to living a sexual life that aligns with your values.

Aligning Sexual Decisions With Core Values

- **Ensures that your actions reflect your deepest beliefs:** When your sexual decisions align with your core values, you are acting in accordance with what truly matters to you. This alignment helps ensure that your behavior is consistent with your personal beliefs, creating a sense of integrity in your actions.
- **Reduces internal conflict, enhances self-respect, and fosters greater satisfaction in intimate connections:** By living in accordance with your values, you minimize internal conflict and self-doubt, leading to enhanced self-respect. This consistency boosts your confidence and deepens the satisfaction you derive from your intimate relationships.
- **Guides behaviors, preferences, and boundaries to create relationships based on mutual respect, trust, and open communication:** Core values shape how you interact with

others and set clear boundaries. This guidance helps establish relationships built on respect and trust, where communication is open and honest, leading to more fulfilling connections.

Contributing to Healthier Relationships and Personal Growth

- **Incorporating your values into your sexual life leads to healthier relationships and supports personal growth:** When your sexual life reflects your core values, it strengthens the quality of your relationships. Living authentically promotes personal growth as you engage in experiences and relationships that are true to who you are.
- **Living authentically allows you to engage in experiences and relationships that resonate with your true self:** Being true to your values ensures that your sexual experiences align with your genuine desires and beliefs. This authenticity enriches your relationships, making them more satisfying and meaningful.
- **This alignment supports long-term satisfaction, emotional well-being, and a deeper connection with yourself and your partners:** Aligning with your values fosters long-term satisfaction and emotional health. It deepens your connection with yourself and enhances the bond you share with your partners, leading to more fulfilling and enduring relationships.

Empowering Navigation of Relationships

- **Commiting to your core values empowers you to navigate relationships with clarity and confidence:** Committing to your values provides a clear sense of direction

in your relationships. This clarity and confidence enable you to make decisions that reflect your true self, leading to more authentic and respectful interactions.
- **Ensuring that your sexual experiences are meaningful and respectful:** By adhering to your core values, you ensure that your sexual experiences are both meaningful and respectful. This alignment helps you engage in relationships that honor your principles and bring genuine fulfillment.
- **Revisiting and refining your values as your life evolves helps build a foundation for personal and relational fulfillment:** As your life circumstances change, revisiting and refining your values keeps you aligned with your evolving self. This ongoing commitment helps build a strong foundation for personal growth and satisfaction in your relationship.

Aligning your sexual decisions with your core values is fundamental for fostering healthy, fulfilling relationships and personal growth. When your actions reflect your deepest beliefs, you create a sense of integrity and consistency that enhances self-respect and reduces internal conflict. This alignment guides your behaviors, preferences, and boundaries. It also ensures that your relationships are built on mutual respect, trust, and open communication.

So explore and incorporate your values into your sexual life to strengthen your relationships and support your personal development. This will allow you to engage in experiences that resonate with your true self. It's a commitment that empowers you to navigate relationships with clarity and confidence, ensuring that your interactions are both meaningful and respectful. Revisiting and refining your values as life evolves, helps you maintain a strong foundation for enduring satisfaction and fulfillment throughout your life. If all that is what you are seeking, you can find it in core values.

CHAPTER TAKEAWAYS

- Identifying personal sexual values brings clarity and direction.
- Understanding past influences helps reshape a fulfilling sex life.
- Aligning sex with values creates deeper satisfaction and confidence.

CONCLUSION

Sex is not just a physical act—it's an emotional and sensory experience that reflects so many aspects of who we are. From our earliest introductions to sex, many of us are taught to focus on technique, performance, and achieving specific outcomes like orgasms. But in reality, the way we view sex now needs to encompass its full complexity. Our sexual identities, desires, and needs are fluid, and they change over time based on experiences, relationships, and personal growth. This is normal, and more importantly, it belongs to you. You have control over your sexuality, and you get to define how it fits into your life.

For some, this shift in mindset might mean letting go of the belief that sex is always tied to intercourse or that it needs to follow a specific script to "count." For others, it could mean embracing new ways to connect with a partner, or even solo exploration. The point is that sex is personal, and there's no right or wrong way to engage with it—as long as it's consensual, respectful, and in alignment with your desires.

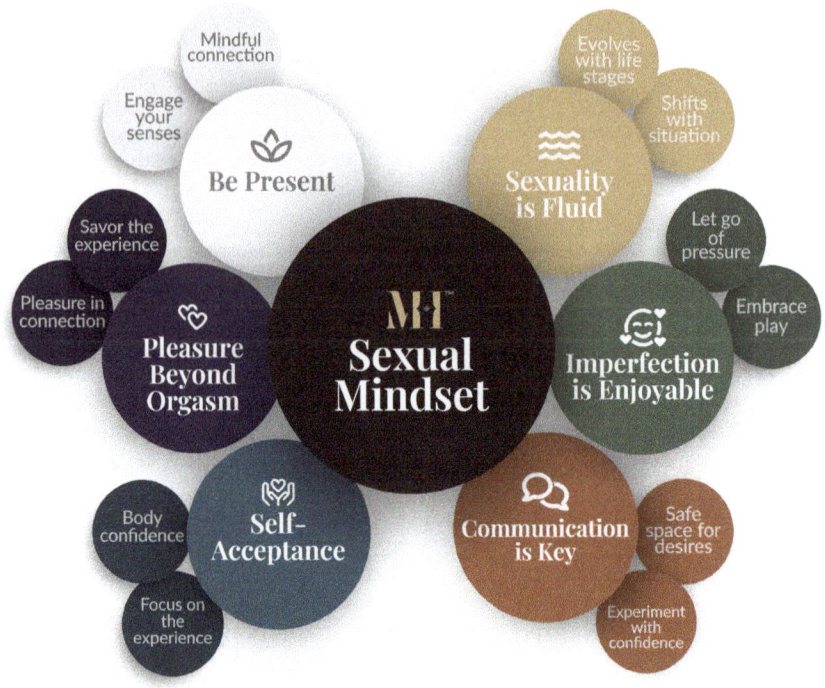

SEXUALITY IS FLUID AND ADAPTIVE

As human beings, we evolve—and so does our relationship with sex. What might have excited or aroused you in your 20s could be different in your 40s or 50s. And that's perfectly okay. Society tends to send us messages that equate sexual worth with youth or stamina, but sexual satisfaction and connection can grow deeper and more meaningful with age. You may find yourself drawn to new kinds of intimacy, slower or more sensual experiences, or even new types of connection that weren't on your radar earlier in life.

This idea of sexual fluidity also allows space for changes in desire. For instance, desire may fluctuate depending on life circumstances—stress, health issues, or emotional well-being can all affect libido. Instead of viewing these changes as problems to "fix," a healthier mindset involves accepting them as part of the natural ebb and flow of your sexuality. When you release the pressure to always be "on," you create space for a more genuine, fulfilling sexual experience.

SEX DOESN'T HAVE TO BE PERFECT TO BE ENJOYABLE

One of the biggest mindset shifts we can make is realizing that sex doesn't need to be perfect to be enjoyable. The reality is that many people get stuck in their heads during sex, worrying about things like performance, timing, or whether they're doing things "right." But sex is not a performance—there's no audience, no judge, and no one keeping score.

True sexual satisfaction comes from embracing the imperfections. Sex can be messy, clumsy, and unexpected, but that's part of its charm. It's not about executing a perfect sequence of events—it's about being in the moment, being connected with your partner, and being kind to yourself when things don't go as planned. When you can let go of expectations and just enjoy the experience for what it is, you'll find that your sexual encounters become more playful, relaxed, and fulfilling.

COMMUNICATION IS THE KEY

Communication is one of the most critical components of a satisfying sex life. It's about more than just talking about sex; it's about creating a safe space where both you and your partner can express desires, boundaries, and fears without judgment. Too often, couples shy away from discussing what they want in bed, either out of embarrassment or the fear of being rejected. But if we can normalize these conversations, we set the foundation for deeper intimacy and trust.

Open communication also allows for more experimentation. When both partners feel safe to express their fantasies or suggest something new, it can lead to greater sexual satisfaction. This doesn't mean every conversation needs to be a deep dive into desires—sometimes it's as simple as asking, "What feels good for you?" or "Is there something new you'd like to try?" These kinds of check-ins keep the sexual dynamic fresh and ensure that both partners are aligned in their pleasure.

MINDFULNESS IN SEX: BEING PRESENT WITH YOURSELF AND YOUR PARTNER

One of the most powerful tools for enhancing your sex life is mindfulness—being fully present in the moment without judgment or distraction. When you slow down and truly focus on what you're feeling, thinking, and experiencing, sex becomes more than just a physical act; it becomes an opportunity to connect deeply with yourself and your partner.

Mindfulness in sex starts with tuning into your emotions. Ask yourself, "How am I feeling right now?" Your emotional state is going to affect your sexual experience, whether you realize it or not. If you're feeling stressed, distracted, or anxious, those feelings will likely carry over into the bedroom. By acknowledging how you feel, you can decide whether you need to address those emotions before diving into sex, or simply be more aware of them during the experience.

Here are some mindful practices that can help shift your sexual mindset:

- **Check In With Your Emotions:** How you feel emotionally can directly impact your sexual experience. If you're stressed, tired, or anxious, that will show up in the bedroom. Acknowledging these emotions can help you be more present during sex. If you're not feeling emotionally aligned, it's okay to pause and address that before diving in. Sometimes a conversation or a moment of relaxation can create the space needed for a better experience.

- **Slow It Down:** Focus on your breath. Slowing down your breathing helps slow your thoughts, bringing you into the present moment. When you're mindful of your breathing, you're also more mindful of the sensations in your body. Slower breathing can reduce performance anxiety, allowing you to focus on pleasure rather than pressure.
- **Stop the Spiral of Worry:** It's easy to get caught in your head during sex, thinking about all the things that could go wrong. "What if I can't keep it up?" "What if my partner isn't satisfied?" These thoughts take you out of the experience and create unnecessary stress. Instead, remind yourself that your partner is with you because they want to be. Focus on the positive aspects of the moment—why you're both there, why you desire each other—and let go of the need for everything to be perfect.
- **Engage Your Senses:** Mindfulness is all about focusing on what's happening right now, and your senses are a great way to ground yourself in the present moment. What can you feel, hear, see, and taste? Engage fully with your body's sensations. Notice the texture of your partner's skin, the sound of their voice or breath, the taste of their kiss. These small details bring you closer to the experience and deepen your connection.

RETHINKING PLEASURE: IT'S MORE THAN JUST THE ORGASM

Another important aspect of this mindset shift is redefining what counts as pleasure. So many of us have been conditioned to believe that sex's primary goal is orgasm, but this focus can overshadow the multitude of other pleasures sex has to offer. Pleasure can come from touch, connection, laughter, or even a shared sense of vulnerability. When you remove orgasm as the end goal, you open yourself up to a broader range of satisfying sexual experiences.

This is where mindfulness really becomes a game-changer. By focusing on each sensation as it happens—without rushing toward the finish line—you create a much more fulfilling experience. Orgasm can still be a part of that, of course, but it no longer has to define success. By reframing pleasure as something that happens throughout the entire sexual experience, you allow yourself to savor every moment.

SELF-ACCEPTANCE AND LETTING GO OF COMPARISON

One of the biggest barriers to a healthy sexual mindset is comparison. Whether it's comparing your body, your performance, or your relationship to unrealistic ideals portrayed in the media, comparison can erode your confidence and take you out of the moment. Learning to accept your body, your desires, and your sexual experiences as they are is essential for a fulfilling sex life.

Sex is not about meeting some external standard; it's about connection, exploration, and pleasure. By letting go of the need to compare yourself to others—whether it's the actors in porn or the expectations you think your partner has—you free yourself to fully engage in your own unique experience of sex.

AUTHOR'S NOTE

At the heart of it all, my goal is to help men take control of their sex lives, shed the pressure of unrealistic expectations, and embrace a more fulfilling, confident, and authentic approach to intimacy. Throughout this book, we've covered the essentials—from understanding your own desires and values to improving communication, managing performance anxiety, and enhancing pleasure through mindfulness and self-awareness. The journey to better sex isn't about achieving perfection; it's about connection—both with yourself and your partner.

Key takeaways from this book include the importance of mindfulness, staying present in the moment rather than getting stuck in your head; the power of communication, ensuring you and your partner are on the same page and comfortable discussing needs and boundaries; and the value of self-awareness, understanding your core values and what truly drives your sexual confidence and satisfaction. We've also explored how to navigate challenges like performance anxiety, redefine masculinity beyond societal expectations, and create an intimate life that reflects who you are—not who you think you should be.

Ultimately, enriching your sex life means letting go of shame, embracing curiosity, and staying open to growth. It's about knowing what you want, communicating it clearly, and approaching every experience with confidence and authenticity. The most satisfying sex life isn't built on technique or stamina—it's built on trust, honesty, and a willingness to keep learning and evolving.

So, as you move forward, I hope you take what you've learned here and put it into action. Stay present, stay honest, and most importantly, stay true to yourself. Your sex life—and your overall well-being—will be better for it.

If, as you finish this book, you find you have additional questions, I urge you to email me at DrMike@MisterHealth.com or take a look at the free resources offered through Mister Health at www.MisterHealth.com.

ABOUT THE AUTHOR

Dr. Michael Stokes—known affectionately by his clients and readers as Dr. Mike—is a licensed professional counselor and AASECT-certified sex therapist who specializes in men's sexual health, intimacy, and overall well-being. With over a decade of clinical experience, Dr. Mike is known for his compassionate, down-to-earth approach that blends expert insight with humor and humanity.

A fierce advocate for breaking down the stigma surrounding men's sexual wellness, Dr. Mike founded his practice to offer a safe, judgment-free space where men can openly talk about their sexual health challenges. His work spans one-on-one coaching, an online community, and a men's wellness center.

He holds multiple state licenses and advanced degrees in counseling and supervision and has helped hundreds of men reclaim confidence in their relationships and redefine their intimate lives. When he's not coaching clients or speaking on sexual health topics nationwide, you'll find Dr. Mike spending time with family or enjoying a strong cup of coffee.

This book is an extension of his mission: to make sexual health conversations accessible, practical, and transformative for every man ready to take control of his wellness journey.

The B Corp Movement

Dear reader,

Thank you for reading this book and joining the Publish Your Purpose community! You are joining a special group of people who aim to make the world a better place.

What's Publish Your Purpose About?
Our mission is to elevate the voices often excluded from traditional publishing. We intentionally seek out authors and storytellers with diverse backgrounds, life experiences, and unique perspectives to publish books that will make an impact in the world.

Beyond our books, we are focused on tangible, action-based change. As a woman- and LGBTQ+-owned company, we are committed to reducing inequality, lowering levels of poverty, creating a healthier environment, building stronger communities, and creating high-quality jobs with dignity and purpose.

As a Certified B Corporation, we use business as a force for good. We join a community of mission-driven companies building a more equitable, inclusive, and sustainable global economy. B Corporations must meet high standards of transparency, social and environmental performance, and accountability as determined by the nonprofit B Lab. The certification process is rigorous and ongoing (with a recertification requirement every three years).

How Do We Do This?
We intentionally partner with socially and economically disadvantaged businesses that meet our sustainability goals. We embrace and encourage our authors and employee's differences in race, age, color, disability, ethnicity, family or marital status, gender identity or expression, language, national origin, physical and mental ability, political affiliation, religion, sexual orientation, socio-economic status, veteran status, and other characteristics that make them unique.

Community is at the heart of everything we do—from our writing and publishing programs to contributing to social enterprise nonprofits like reSET (https://www.resetco.org/) and our work in founding B Local Connecticut.

We are endlessly grateful to our authors, readers, and local community for being the driving force behind the equitable and sustainable world we are building together.

To connect with us online, or publish with us,
visit us at www.publishyourpurpose.com.

Elevating Your Voice,

Jenn T Grace

Jenn T. Grace
Founder, Publish Your Purpose

www.ingramcontent.com/pod-product-compliance
Lightning Source LLC
Chambersburg PA
CBHW061252230426
43665CB00026B/2912